THE
LANGUAGE OF LEARNING

THE
LANGUAGE OF LEARNING:
The Preschool Years

Marion Blank, Ph.D.
College of Medicine and Dentistry of New Jersey
Rutgers Medical School
Piscataway, New Jersey

Susan A. Rose, Ph.D.
Department of Psychiatry
Albert Einstein College of Medicine
Bronx, New York

Laura J. Berlin, M.S.
Specialist Certificate in School Psychological Services
Department of Psychiatry
Albert Einstein College of Medicine
Bronx, New York

GRUNE & STRATTON
A Subsidiary of Harcourt Brace Jovanovich, Publishers
New York   San Francisco   London

Library of Congress Cataloging in Publication Data

Blank, Marion.
    The language of learning.

    Bibliography
    Includes index.
    1. Language arts (Preschool)   2. Children—Language.
I. Rose, Susan A., joint author.   II. Berlin, Laura J.,
joint author.   III. Title [DNLM: 1. Child, Preschool.
2. Child development.   3. Language development.
4. Learning—In infancy and childhood. WS105.5.C8 B641'L]
LB1140.5.L3B55   372.6   78-02236
ISBN 0-8089-1058-2

Grune & Stratton, Inc.
111 Fifth Avenue
New York, New York 10003

Distributed in the United Kingdom by
Academic Press, Inc. (London) Ltd.
24/28 Oval Road, London NW 1

Library of Congress Catalog Number 78-02236
International Standard Book Number 0-8089-1058-2

Printed in the United States of America

to our families

Contents

48144

Acknowledgments

Many people and institutions have been invaluable in helping us carry out the work reported here. First we would like to thank the staff and directors of the following nursery schools, day care centers, and kindergartens in New York City and its suburbs for their generous cooperation: Alcott Montessori Schools, Bronxdale Day Care Center, Bronx River Day Care Center, Castle Hill Children's Center, Claremont Day Care Center, Crawford Day Care Center, Creative Day School, East Tremont Children's Center, Hebrew Academy of Pelham Parkway, Mount Tom Day School, NAACP Day Care Center, Pengilly Day Nursery, the New York City public schools, Ridge Street Day School, Seven Corners Children's Center, Soundview Day Care Center, St. John's Nursery, St. Paul's Nursery, Victory Day Care Center, and Webster Day Care Center. We are deeply indebted to the children with whom we worked and to their parents who permitted them to participate in the study.

We want to thank our dedicated research staff members Susan Berenzweig, Merelyn Dolins, Frances Goldenberg, Marilyn Markowitz, Patricia Pattie, Frances Solomon, Irene Spalter, and Marilyn Tartaglia. Their commitment to the project, sensitivity to children, and intelligent work have contributed inestimably to this project. Most particularly, we want to express our gratitude to Rita Rapp who, in addition to being a superb worker, stayed on to help us complete the research when funds for the project were exhausted.

Book writing always entails an endless series of revisions. The rewriting process was greatly aided by our colleagues who had the tedious chore of reading the various drafts and offered cogent comments and criticisms. We particularly would like to thank Doris Allen, Herbert Kohn, Bonnie Markham, and Susan Rubenstein. We are also most grateful to Dorothy Caplan for her typing and retyping of the seemingly endless copies.

This project came into existence only because of the generous support of the William T. Grant Foundation and the National Institutes of Mental Health (Grants

5 KO2 MH 10749 and MH 21051). It is with heartfelt appreciation that we would like to thank, most especially, Mr. Philip Sapir, director of the William T. Grant Foundation, for the trust, warmth, and interest that he has shown throughout this endeavor. This brief acknowledgment falls far short of our gratitude to him for his major role in the development of this work.

Marion Blank
Susan A. Rose
Laura J. Berlin

Preface

The work presented in this book can be described from a number of vantage points. Its essence, however, seems most effectively and succinctly captured in the dialogue from a cartoon involving two young children.

As they are trudging up a hill, the first child says, "Today in school, the teacher explained all about inflation."

The second child, his attention piqued, asks, "Well, what is inflation?"

To this, the first replies, "All I said was she explained it. I didn't say I understood it."

(From Bud Blake, King Features Syndicate, Inc., 1977.)

THE
LANGUAGE OF LEARNING

1

Teaching Thinking in the Preschool?

In the past several years, preschools increasingly have taken on the ambitious and difficult task of teaching the higher level intellectual activities that are valued by our society. It is now rare to find a program that does not see as one of its roles the enhancement of thinking, problem solving, concept formation, and reasoning (Parker, 1972; Robison, 1977). Although few would contest these goals, there is considerable controversy about the methods by which they might be attained. Programs vary greatly in their beliefs as to the amount of structuring that should be offered, the types of materials that should be made available, and the quality of teacher–child interaction that should be fostered.

Regardless of differences in orientation, one factor that almost all programs share (with the notable exception of Montessori) is the importance placed on the verbal exchange that occurs between the teacher and the child. Even in programs in which "the emphasis is not on teaching but on the teacher's assisting in the learning process," the teacher will be asked "to develop the children's mental process by posing questions and by helping the child to verbalize and formulate his ideas and thoughts" (Beller, 1973, p. 566). This approach is illustrated in a recent report from a leading program that is geared to capitalizing on child-initiated activities. Although the teachers are advised not to be intrusive, it is nevertheless expected that they will develop numerical concepts by asking questions such as, *are there as many crackers as there are children.* Similarly, it is expected that they will foster the recognition of attributes by asking questions such as, *can you find something that is red and made of wood* (Banet, 1975 p. 11).

These examples are not unique. They are typical of the complex language demands that are used in all types of preschool programs to facilitate the child's intellectual growth. The reliance on language can easily be

1

understood. In part, it represents the downward extension into the preschool of techniques that have long been used with older children (Bellack et al., 1966) and in part, it represents the degree to which verbal activities permeate the human exchange. Language is a remarkably versatile skill and it is rare to encounter a setting in which it does not play an important role. Thus, the prevalence of language in the preschool is not, and should not be, surprising.

What is surprising is the paucity of information that exists about the characteristics, range, and purposes of the language used in the teacher–child exchange. There is little information about what actually occurs (Gordon & Jester, 1973) and even less information about what should occur if the child's learning is to be facilitated.[1] In place of explicit knowledge there exists a mélange of implicit ideas and techniques that are often drawn from a disparate set of philosophies. Rousseau's influence can be seen in the emphasis on the teacher's response to the child's initiations; Piaget's influence can be seen in the emphasis on concepts such as space, time, and seriation, and Hume's influence can be seen in the emphasis on the direct teaching of skills and values (Beller, 1973).

The diverse influences need not necessarily mean that preschool teaching is inappropriate or ineffective. It is clear from the many reported studies that children are affected by their preschool experience (Beller, 1973; Gordon & Jester, 1973). It is also clear that there is an increasing number of efforts to specify the components that affect the children's behavior. For example, it is common now to categorize the teacher's behavior into groupings such as "offers a purely verbal comment," "accompanies a visual or auditory aid with a verbal comment," and "requests elaboration from the child" (Miller & Dyer, 1975).

Although this type of coding has served to categorize some of the teacher's behaviors, it falls far short of the level of analysis that is required if we are to have an in-depth understanding of the verbal encounters that occur between teacher and child.

The level of analysis that we have in mind can be illustrated by referring to the questions cited earlier (i.e., *are there as many crackers as there are children* and *can you find something that is red and made of wood*).

---

[1]Because of the increasing recognition of the importance of language, a number of investigators have directed their efforts towards studying the verbal interactions in the classroom. (See Amidon & Hough, 1967; Barnes et al., 1969; Bellack et al., 1966; Bennett & Jordon, 1975; Candlin, 1972; Cazden et al., 1972; Coulthard, 1974; Flanders, 1970; Simon & Boyer, 1968; and Soar & Soar, 1976 for illustrations of these studies.) This work has not been directed at the preschool-age child, however, even though the preschool has been recognized as being of paramount importance in laying the foundation for higher level intellectual activities.

These questions differ on a number of dimensions. They involve different grammatical structures, they refer to different concepts, and they demand the analyses of different materials. Because of the way they have been designed, most current rating systems would place these two questions into a single category such as "solicits ideas and information" (Gordon & Jester, 1973, p. 195). This type of categorization obliterates many of the crucial distinctions in the teacher–child communication and in so doing, leaves us uninformed about the specific ways in which language can affect children's intellectual activities. If progress is to be made, it is essential to develop a model that identifies, with precision, the key factors that under-lie productive teacher–child interchanges.

There are good reasons for shying away from an effort of this kind. Because language is simultaneously multidimensional and little under-stood, any attempt to define even a single sentence turns out to be a difficult and controversial chore. For example, when a teacher makes the very typical request, *find all the curved blocks and put them in one pile,* should this request be judged on its grammatical complexity, on the par-ticular concepts or referents it contains, or on the activity that it is de-signed to elicit? Because of this ambiguity, any effort at specification will depend not solely on "facts," but on one's philosophy as to how the "facts" should be interpreted (Kuhn, 1962). It can therefore be easily chal-lenged on the grounds that it is speculative and biased.

The failure to mount an effort to systematize the language of instruction has an even greater drawback. In the absence of such an effort, we will continue to lack the precise information necessary if teachers are to go beyond the vague notions that they are currently forced to use. In essence, they have been assigned a tremendously ambitious task, but they have been given few of the tools necessary for carrying out their assignment. The presentation of a system that defines the language of instruction has the potential of bringing forth some of the information necessary if teachers are to be helped to reach their objectives. It is for this reason that the work to be presented here contains as its first goal the development of a model that defines the language of effective instruction. Essentially, we will attempt to define what we believe the teacher can and ought to be saying to the child in the effort to have that child gain maximally from the school experience.

Although they are considerable, the greatest problems with regard to the language of the preschool do not stem from the speculations that are inherent in model building. Rather, they stem from the age range of the children in question. Because schooling is so highly valued in our society, the general feeling has been "the earlier, the better." As a result of this philosophy, insufficient attention has been devoted to the potential conflict that exists between the unavoidable demands of the formal teaching setting and the developmental limitations of young children. Even though the precise demands of the teaching situation are not known, what is known is sufficient to indicate that children must possess a number of complex prerequisite skills if they are simply to cope with the exchanges in which they are involved. For instance, to refer once more to the *are there as many crackers as there are children* illustration, it seems clear that from the teacher's perspective the goal is to develop one-to-one correspondence. If the children are to deal with the idea that the teacher has in mind, they must be able to draw a number of sophisticated verbal and conceptual skills (e.g., they must understand the phrase "as many as," be able to engage in a comparison of children with crackers, and so on). In other words, the posing of this question is predicated on the assumption that children possess these prerequisite skills. If this assumption were not held, the teacher would never be encouraged to ask these questions. Despite the assumption—and it is prevalent—we have no knowledge whether young children have already mastered the necessary skills.

The situation is made even more complex because the instructional process is, at heart, a special form of communication. We are often so focused on the concepts and skills that we wish to maximize *within* the child that we often fail to notice that the essence of the teaching experience is not within the child alone. Rather, it is in the exchange that is taking place *between* the teacher and child. Although the communication situation in the classroom may be different from others (e.g., communication among peers, communication between parent and child, and so forth), it nevertheless entails many of the same demands (Kearsley, 1976). As in the illustrations cited here, for example, the teacher commonly makes a request that the children are expected to meet. Regardless of how sensitively and appropriately the teacher has phrased the question to match the children's needs, the situation still requires that they attend to an idea formulated by another person, express themselves in a way that meets the constraints imposed in a complex question, and integrate this information into the sequence of events so that it furthers their knowledge and understanding.

While information on children's communication skills is scarce, the available reports present a divided and confusing picture. Some experts see young children as possessing considerable skill in communication (Bates, 1976; Blank, 1974; Garvey & Hogan, 1973; Isaacs, 1930; Schatz & Gelman, 1973). According to this view, children of preschool age can:

produce mutually responsive speech, well beyond simple exchanges . . . as early as age 3 children have already worked out, in the way they make requests or respond to them, well-advanced social–cognitive patterns or

schemata that systematically use conventional language and vocabu-
lary. Language is not only a means for, but an important aspect of, social
interaction. (Krasner, 1975, p. 3, summarizing research by Garvey)

In contrast, other investigators see children as being severely limited in
their ability to use language in any meaningful or sustained social interchange (Dale, 1972; Krauss & Glucksberg, 1969; Piaget, 1969; Stevenson,
1972). One specialist in children's language development summarizes the
young child's performance in the following way:

The Russian children's poet, Kornei Chukovsky, calls the preschool child
"a linguistic genius" and the accolade is deserved if we think only of the
acquisition of grammar. However, the child is an uneven genius. If we set
him a task of communication, even a very elementary one, then the
genius gives way to the child. . . . As speaker, for example, his perfor-
mance is likely to show the following sorts of defects: 1. Difficulty in
relying exclusively on language. . . . 2. Egocentricism. He is likely to use
terms and draw upon experiences that his interlocutor does not
share. . . . 3. Failure to analyze the given information according to the
problem. . . . (Brown, 1968a, pp. v –vi)

All who are familiar with young children can almost certainly call to mind
examples that support both viewpoints. At times we have all tried to speak
with children only to find them talking in a way that leaves us puzzled; at
other times, the same children are responsive and totally comprehensible.
In that sense, both views are "right," for each has extracted a component
in the complexity that is a child. Most relevant for our purposes, however,
is the degree to which they are right; or more accurately, which view is
most characteristic of children in the school situation? If the most common picture of young children is the one in which they are strong in their
use of language, then we cannot only rely on the verbal component in the
instructional process—we may actually be able to use that component in
far more fruitful ways than has been the practice to date. If, however, the
most common picture is one in which the children are weak in verbal
communication, then it appears that the language of instruction would at
best have to be severely modified. Indeed, if children typically have as
severe difficulties in communication as has sometimes been reported,
then the possibility exists that verbally based instruction may not even be
feasible for the preschool period.

These comments are not designed to suggest that the only benefits of
the preschool are those that derive from verbally based teaching. Many
other gains can accrue from the preschool experience (e.g., the opportunity for social interaction with peers, the availability of well-designed materials, and so forth). Rather, what we are suggesting is that despite its

long-accepted use, it has not been established that the language of instruction can be comprehended by the young child. Regardless of what we think we are achieving or what we would like to achieve in offering statements, suggestions, or questions to the child, we may in fact be offering little if the child is not proficient in the skills that are needed to be a full participant in the verbal exchange.

Resolution of this issue is particularly crucial at this time when preschools have come to serve as a major vehicle for reducing the high rate of school failure among children from poverty backgrounds (e.g., Head Start). This use of the preschool represents an effort to offer children services that will enhance their chances for later academic success. But if questions exist about the verbal skills of the preschooler in general, then even more questions exist about these skills in children from poverty backgrounds. While this issue is hotly debated, the evidence suggests that these children experience particularly marked problems in the language required for school success. (See Bereiter & Engelmann, 1966, Bruck & Tucker, 1974, Cazden et al., 1972; Criper & Davies, 1977; Deutsch et al., 1968; Higgins, 1976; Lawton, 1968; and Tough, 1977 for illustrations and evaluations of the language skills of young disadvantaged children.) The existence of these problems suggests that even if verbally based instruction is found practicable, the actual exchanges that take place may have to be carefully tailored if they are to deal with the problems that have characterized the school experiences of children from the lower socioeconomic classes.

The problems that we have been considering here with regard to the young child's developmental limitations have determined the second goal of this book. Specifically, we wish to study whether, and to what extent, young children have the abilities to deal with a verbally based process of instruction. In an effort to answer this question, we have developed a comprehensive test for preschool-age children that is designed to assess their skills in verbal exchange with a teacher. The content and organization of the test is based on the model of instruction that we have developed in line with the first goal, cited earlier.

This book presents the work that we have carried out in developing and applying both the model and the test. Because a number of varied issues are covered, it seems useful to present an overview of the material that is to follow.

The work is divided into two volumes. The remainder of the first volume is organized as follows:

Chapter 2 presents the model that we have developed to characterize the language of the instructional process that is necessary to facilitate children's learning.

Chapter 3 outlines the test that we have designed to assess young children's skill in dealing with the demands of the instructional situation.

Chapter 4 describes the sample of 288 children who have been given the test. The sample is distributed evenly over the age range of 36 to 71 months. Because of the role that social class factors have been reported to play in school language, the sample has been selected so that half the children come from lower-class and half from middle-class backgrounds.

Chapter 5 outlines the major findings of the children's performance on the test. The analysis is geared to answering two major questions.

1. Do preschool-age children possess the language skills needed for engaging in productive verbal exchange with the teachers?
2. If they do possess such skills, to what extent are they equivalent in preschool-age children from middle- and lower-class backgrounds?

Chapter 6 is directed at illustrating the ways in which the findings can be used so as to enhance teacher–child interchange in the preschool.

The companion volume to this book, *Preschool Language Assessment Instrument: The Language of Learning in Practice,* presents an experimental version of the test. It is designed for use by psychologists, teachers, and other specialists who wish to assess children's skills in school-based language. It represents a shortened and simplified version of the comprehensive test that has been used for the analysis to be presented here. Despite the modifications, the shortened test taps essentially the same language processes and yields similar information about the children's skills.

2

A Model of Classroom Language

SELECTING A FRAMEWORK

We have set out to study the language of the preschool that fosters higher level intellectual activities. As in other human interactions, language in this setting encompasses a diverse and complex realm. The critical issue that arises, therefore, is how to best characterize the range of language activities within a finite and meaningful set of categories.

There are several possible approaches to this problem. At one end of the continuum one may try to be as empirical as possible and survey the interactions in a number of classrooms. The hope is that from these observations one can extract the basic features of productive interchange (McNeil & Popham, 1973). Although this approach is commonly used in educational studies, it contains several disadvantages. First, preschool programs vary widely on a range of dimensions. As a result, a large number of programs would have to be surveyed in order to ensure that a full set of behaviors has been adequately sampled. Second, in any school day numerous exchanges take place that are not concerned with intellectual goals (e.g., housekeeping routines, disciplinary procedures, and so forth). Furthermore, even among the exchanges that are designed to stimulate thinking, there are in fact many arbitrary and often counterproductive demands that the school uses "simply to symbolize its capacity for authority over its charges" (Olson, 1967, p. 13). Considerable sifting of data is therefore necessary in order to sort out the interactions that mediate intellectual activities from those that do not. Third, even when the nonrelevant encounters are eliminated there is still the problem of imposing a framework that will permit the numerous interactions that remain to be organized in a meaningful way. The empirical approach therefore seems only to delay

and, at times, even disguise the conceptual organization that must ultimately be imposed if the complex behaviors under study are to be understood.

Because of these disadvantages and because the conceptual organization is so primary, we have chosen to begin by formulating a model at the
outset of our endeavor. Our goal is to develop a conceptual scheme by
which to identify and systematize the essential elements in productive
teacher–child exchanges. In attempting to accomplish this goal, we have
elected to combine two basic features of the preschool, (1) the generally
accepted intellectual aims of preschool education and (2) our view of
classroom instruction. The aims to which we are referring are the ones
embodied in terms such as helping the child to *observe sharply, identify
attributes, associate like attributes, classify, anticipate next steps, reason
inductively,* and *make deductions* (Robison, 1977, p. 347). The view of
instruction to which we are referring is the one presented in Chapter 1.
Essentially, we perceive the classroom as a communication situation in
which the teacher's verbalizations with the children are designed to lead
them to the aforementioned aims.

An interesting, albeit rarely considered, phenomenon in education is
that the various aims of instruction are expressed through different language formulations. For example, the aim of leading the child to *observe
sharply* is likely to be expressed in a question such as, **what . . . did you
see there**; the aim of associating *like attributes* is likely to be expressed
in a request such as, **put all the . . . that are the same in one pile**; and the
aim of *anticipating next steps* is likely to be expressed in a question such
as, **what will happen if . . .**

Although the linguistic formulations vary with the educational aims, the
relationship is not that of one-to-one correspondence. The same aim can
be expressed in several different ways [e.g., *what . . . do you see, what
(color, shape, and so on) were they,* and *what was the difference between
the . . .*] can all serve to foster observation. Conversely, the same linguistic
formulations can serve several different aims (e.g., *what will happen if . . .*
may enhance anticipation, imagery, and prediction). Nevertheless, there
tends to be a fairly high degree of association between the teaching aims
and the language used. To a considerable extent, similar aims are represented through similar language formulations while different aims are
represented through different language formulations.

Words referring to specific content, that is, the particular material being
discussed, have intentionally been omitted from the preceding examples
in an effort to highlight the fact that the same formulations are used regardless of the content being discussed. The independence of language
from content is a major advantage in any effort to build a model. Were

language formulations to vary markedly according to the content under discussion, the situation would be one of overwhelming complexity. If we consider even a single day within the preschool, for example, we can easily find that a teacher has planned the curriculum so that it will include a trip to the supermarket to buy food for a party to be held the next day, the reading of a story designed to help children become aware of social relationships, the making of lemonade as a special treat during juice time, the setting aside of a block of time to teach prepositions such as *inside* and *above,* and finally the use of a "show-and-tell" period to allow the children the opportunity to speak before their peers. If the basic language formulations differed significantly in each of these activities (i.e., if the language formulations needed to talk about a trip to the supermarket were different from those needed in a lesson on prepositions), then it would be necessary to develop a different model of instruction for each content area. Because of the link between the aims and the language of instruction, there is no need to focus on the differences among topics. Regardless of the topic being considered, the same language formulations can be applied. The formulations will vary not according to differences in content, but rather according to differences in the aims that the teacher wishes to attain.

Because the focus in early education has been almost exclusively directed toward the aims that are to be fostered, little attention has been given to the relationship that exists between the aims and the language. Indeed, in many cases language itself has been seen as one of the aims. That is, it is seen as one of the areas to be fostered within the children. Just as one attempts to enhance children's observational and reasoning skills, one attempts to enhance their language skills (e.g., their concepts, sequencing, expressive language, and so forth). The emphasis on language (as a skill to be fostered within the child) has contributed to the neglect that has been shown to the role of language as a tool that the teacher employs in achieving the aims of the instructional process. In our view, the range of language formulations that must be used in fostering the different aims represents the key to understanding the verbal component of the instructional process. If the formulations can be defined and systematized, we will have a picture of the repertoire of language skills that teachers must be trained to use if they are to cover a gamut of intellectual activities. The remainder of this chapter will be devoted to the system that we have developed in an effort to arrive at this picture.

A MODEL OF DISCOURSE

Although the relationship between the aims and the language of instruction has not been emphasized in studies with young children, investigators working with older students have begun to consider them (Barnes et al.,

1969; Candlin, 1972), and we have been guided by the ideas that these investigators have put forth. In particular, we have been influenced by James Moffett (1968), an educator who is concerned with showing how language may be used as fully and flexibly as possible in order to enhance the students' knowledge and understanding. The central notion in Moffett's view of language is that verbal behavior is distorted when it is divided into traditionally accepted categories such as grammar, vocabulary, or concepts. Instead, in a notion that has particularly attracted us to his work, he sees language above all as a medium of communication—as a means whereby information is transmitted between the teacher and the child.

Using the concept of communication as its core, Moffett goes on to develop a model of what the communication process ought to be if it is to stimulate children's intellectual development. Because Moffett is concerned with much older students, the model is not directly applicable for our purposes. With suitable modifications, however, the model can be adapted for the preschooler, and this is what we have strived to achieve.

Moffett's model contains three components which, at first glance, are disarmingly simple. First, there are the participants who are speaking and listening to one another (the speaker–listener dyad); second, there is the topic or subject which the participants are discussing; and third, there is the level of the discussion. At all times the components in any conversation are interrelated in that the speaker and the listener are talking to each other about the topic and are discussing it at a particular level of complexity. Nevertheless, for purposes of exposition, it is necessary to discuss each component separately. We would like to begin our outline of the model by focusing on the third component, the level of the discussion, as it most closely corresponds to the cognitive aims that are at the heart of the preschool effort.

The Level of Discussion

We will begin the analysis of the level of the discussion by imagining a class in which the teacher and children are preparing a batch of cookies. As in any interchange a variety of ideas will be raised at various points as the cookie making progresses. Since we are focused on the teachers' role, we will confine ourselves here to the comments and questions that they might put forth. Some likely ones are:

What is this? *(referring to the flour)*
What things do you see on the table?
Now we'll need a bowl to mix all these things together.
What shape is the bowl?
Tell me what we put in the bowl before we added the egg.
Show me the part of the egg that we don't eat.

Why don't we eat that part?
What will happen to the cookies when we put them in the oven?
Oh, look how they are spreading out!
I'd like to have one.
We'll need to use a potholder because otherwise we'll burn our hands.
Please give me the potholder.
Let's think of some other things that we can bake in the oven.

At first glance, the most salient feature of the teacher's comments and questions is their great diversity. This is a natural consequence of the wide number of aims that the teacher is trying to meet. (See Robison, 1977, and Sigel & Cocking, 1977, for illustrative lists of the aims that have been set for teachers.) Although the diversity of the verbal formulations is important, of even greater importance for our purposes is the level of complexity of the formulations. For instance, a request such as, *tell me what we put in the bowl before we added the egg,* will almost certainly be more demanding for a young child than a question such as, *what is this.* It is the differential complexity of the demands that we call the "level of the discussion." Although the complexity of the formulations has not been given much consideration, it represents a vital parameter of the teacher's language. In general, the advice to teachers is to ask increasingly complex questions since these are deemed to serve as *"investigators, activators,* and *organizers* of mental operations" (Sigel & Cocking, 1977, p. 213). The commonly held view is that the more complex the question, the more likely it is to produce higher level mental activities. It is largely on the basis of this belief that teachers are discouraged from asking certain questions (e.g., questions demanding convergent thinking) since such questions are deemed less likely to demand active engagement of the child's mind.

Although complex levels of demand are deemed desirable, there is little systematic knowledge about the specific levels of complexity that any demand entails. As in the examples offered earlier (e.g., *tell me what we put in the bowl before we added the egg,* versus *what is this),* intuitive judgments can be made about selected instances. There is, however, no overall explicit framework for judging the total array of formulations that teachers use. It is our belief that an understanding of the levels of complexity is the key to understanding the language of instruction. Accordingly, this issue is the one towards which we have focused our efforts.

A Scale of Abstraction for the Preschooler

In attempting to extract the features that determine complexity for a child, major problems arise because language varies on so many dimensions (e.g., sentences differ in grammatical structure, vocabulary, length, and conceptual complexity). In different sentences, any one of these dimensions may stand out as particularly salient (e.g., one sentence may be judged as difficult because of its grammatical structure, another because of its vocabulary, and so forth). As a result, there is a strong tendency to shift the frame of reference in comparing any set of verbal formulations. If we are to construct a coherent picture of the total, it is essential that we do not shift the frame of reference but rather *select a single dimension against which all the teacher's formulations can be assessed.*

We believe that a suitable dimension is available in a concept that we have termed "perceptual-language distance." This term has been chosen to reflect the two types of information that any discussion involves. First, there is the material being discussed (for ease of communication, the material is represented by the term "perceptual" in the perceptual-language distance rubric). Second, there is the language that the teacher uses to direct the child's analysis of the material (again, for ease of communication, the teacher's language is represented by the term "language" in the preceding rubric). According to the way it is formulated, the teacher's language can be quite close to or quite removed from the material. During a trip to the zoo, for example, a teacher could point to some animals (a tiger and a giraffe) and ask, "What are the names of those animals?" Alternatively, he or she could point to the same animals and say, "What is the same about both of them?" Although both questions deal with material that is before the child, the demands involve different relationships between the perceptual and verbal components. In the former, an almost one-to-one correspondence holds between what the child sees and says; in the latter, the language no longer has this tight relationship to the perception. Instead, the child must think of a verbal response that is appropriate to the two different objects but not immediately evident in either. As such, in the request for a judgment of similarity there is a considerably greater distance between the perception and the language than there is in the first question.

These different types of relationships are what we are attempting to capture in the term "perceptual-language distance." As the distance between the material and the language widens, increasingly greater demands are placed on the children to abstract the information from the material that is available to them. We have attempted to capture the increasing demands for abstraction in a scale that contains four main levels. At the lowest level of abstraction there is a minimal distance between the language and the perception. As the demand for abstraction increases, the distance between the two components increases as well, so that at the highest level of separation the children are required to evaluate their perceptions and arrive at levels of judgment and reasoning that are based on, but go beyond, the specific information available at the moment. The increasing separation between the perception and the language is shown in the titles given for each level of abstraction: *Matching Perception, Selective Analysis of Perception, Reordering Perception, and Reasoning about Perception.* A full discussion of the reasons for our selecting perceptual-language distance as the key dimension is not feasible here, for it would require extensive elaboration of the nature of the child's cognitive and linguistic skills. We will try to highlight, however, the major factors that have led us to view the problem in the way that we do.

The Interplay between Language and Cognition in Children

A theme that has become increasingly important in recent developmental studies is the idea that young children's verbal skills cannot be considered apart from their already well-developed sensorimotor skills. Well before they speak, children have learned numerous ways of coping with the world. They can recognize people, manipulate objects, imitate things that they have seen and heard, and solve simple problems such as overcoming obstacles that block their way to a desired object. Thus, when language is acquired it enters an organism with a firmly established set of behaviors. For the most part, the language at first seems simply to become part of the available nonverbal patterns.

Young children, for example, have long known what a ball is. They know that it is something that can be rolled, bounced, and thrown. When the label "ball" is acquired, it does not serve to change their understanding of the object. Rather, the situation seems to be the other way around. Children are prone to learn a word such as "ball" because it represents an important, attractive, and comprehensible object in their lives. These ideas are summarized in the following quotation:

> *During the period before he speaks, the child is busy building up a repertoire of basic cognitive concepts—ways of organizing and understanding his experiences. His task in acquiring language is to discover the linguistic devices by means of which such concepts can be expressed. In other words, acquiring language consists in large part of learning how to map or translate from one representational system (the child's prelinguistic conceptual notions) into another (language). (Bowerman, 1976, p. 101)*

As this statement suggests, early language follows and basically mirrors the concepts that the child has already developed.[1] Furthermore, as in the

---

[1]This issue is currently being explored extensively in psycholinguistics. Interested readers might find the following references of particular value: Blank & Allen, 1976; Bowerman, 1974; Brown, 1973; MacNamara, 1972; Nelson, 1974; Schlesinger, 1974.

ball example, these concepts are reflections of the child's sensorimotor style of dealing with the world. A major characteristic of that style is the child's attraction to salient impressions. In the words of a leading Soviet scientist, the child is "a slave . . . of the physical properties of the stimulus" (Luria, 1960, p. 374).

It has been suggested that children's attraction to perceptual salience is responsible for the fact that many of their earliest words tend to be nouns and verbs. Nouns frequently represent objects or things, and verbs frequently represent actions. Since objects (such as ball) and actions (such as run) are salient for children, it is only natural that their first words reflect the attraction that these stimuli hold for them. (See MacNamara, 1972, for an extended treatment of this topic.)

This discussion may seem far afield from the language of the classroom. The distance, however, is not that great. Many of the questions typically put to children in the preschool are basically tapping into this level of abstraction. Questions or directives such as *what is this, find me a . . .,* or *what do you see* require that the children map their language onto the perception that is currently capturing, or has just captured, their attention. Because the language and perception are so closely meshed at this point, this level of abstraction has been termed *Matching Perception.*

There is a critical difference that should not be lost between children spontaneously using a word such as "ball" and using the same word in response to a question such as, *what is this.* In the former situation the children are using their language when and where they like. In the latter situation, although the same verbal and perceptual skills are involved, there is the *additional component of communication.* The children are now willing and able to call on their intellectual skills *to mesh with the mind of another person.* They are, of course, only at the very beginning of this process. Nevertheless, their behavior shows that they are becoming accessible to learning through talking about experiences with others. As a result, they have embarked on a path that is unique to the human community, that is *the use of language as a way of transmitting information from one generation to the next.*

We have spent considerable time in elaborating on the first level of abstraction because it provides a foundation against which to evaluate the subsequent features that we have isolated in the child's growing communication skills. Gradually, language is used in ways that reflect increasing distance between the perceptual style with which the children view the world and the language they apply to these perceptions. The three additional levels of our scale are designed to encompass this development. The second level of abstraction—*Selective Analysis of Perception*—is intended to represent those demands that require children to resist their attraction to global perceptions and instead respond selectively to different aspects or features of the situation. (See Donaldson & Wales, 1970, for a discussion of the child's development of attribution.) Some typical demands that can be placed on children at this level are, on the one hand, requests for them to attend to attributes (e.g., *what color is this* or *what shape is this*) and, on the other hand, requests to integrate several different elements into a unified idea (e.g., *what is happening in this picture*). Demands at this level are more abstract than those at the first level because they require the children to attend in a more controlled and detailed manner. Nevertheless, these demands do not require them to move beyond the perceptual information that is or has been made available.

The third level of abstraction—*Reordering Perception*—represents a major change in the relationship between the children's language and their sensorimotor style of responding. With demands at this level, the children are required specifically to reject the perceptual or action characteristics that have had such appeal for them and instead internally manipulate or rework their experiences so that these experiences are in accord with the verbal demands of the task. Luria's description (1961) of young children's struggles with the negative term is an instance of this type of verbal demand. For example, children may be given a rubber bulb which they are asked to press when they hear the word *press,* and avoid pressing when they hear the command, *do not press.* This is a difficult achievement for young children. When they hear any command, they are impelled to act; thus the command, *do not press,* leads them to press. The appropriate response, of course, requires that the action be inhibited. As the children begin to attend more closely to language, they become capable of inhibiting their action, for the meaning of *not* overcomes the impulse to act. At this point the language is no longer mirroring but is now serving to control or reorganize the perception and action.

The fourth and final level of abstraction—which seems most aptly captured by the term *Reasoning about Perception* —deals with demands that lead children to think about what may, might, could, or would happen to materials. At this level the children must not only use but clearly go beyond the perceptual information so as to reflect on its implications and interpret its significance. Many of the "why" questions that children themselves typically ask (e.g., *why don't ships sink*) reflect this level of abstraction. (See Chukovsky, 1963, and Isaacs, 1930, for examples of this type of verbal mastery in young children.)

Figure 2-1 is a graphic representation of the scale of abstraction that we have been discussing. It is designed to show the increasing separation that exists between the material that is available to the child and the language formulation that the teacher may impose about different aspects of the material. The divisions between the levels are not sharp; rather, one level

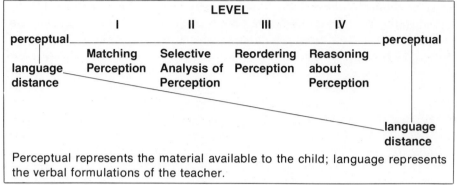

Figure 2-1.   *The perceptual-language distances underlying the scale of abstraction.*

flows into the other in a smooth progression. Nevertheless, the levels are deemed to reflect the qualitatively different demands for abstraction that are placed on the child in the different language formulations which teachers use.

An Illustration of the Scale of Abstraction

Because of its schematic nature, any model is far removed from the rich behavior that it is designed to represent. Therefore, the reader's reaction at this point may well be one of skepticism about the extent to which the four levels of abstraction encompass the wide variety of demands that teachers impose in their efforts to enhance children's cognitive skills. The next chapter elaborates on the relationship between the model and the discourse demands. It indicates that the levels that have been outlined do serve to categorize an extremely broad range of behaviors. Rather than awaiting that discussion, it seems useful at this point to reexamine the hypothetical example about cookie making that was presented earlier in the chapter.

As was indicated there, the demands cover a range of ideas. What we will do here is organize the demands according to the levels of abstraction that they represent. The first level of abstraction is *Matching Perception.* Some of the teacher's verbalizations that fit into this level are:

What is this?
What things do you see on the table?
I'd like to have one.
Please give me the potholder.

At the second level of abstraction, *Selective Analysis of Perception,* some of the key demands are:

Table 2-1   *An Overview of the Scale of Abstraction for Preschool Discourse*

I	Matching Perception	reporting and responding to salient information	What things do you see on table?
II	Selective Analysis of Perception	reporting and responding to delineated and less salient cues	What shape is the bowl?
III	Reordering Perception	using language to restructure perceptual input and inhibit predisposing responses	Show me the part of the egg that we don't eat.
IV	Reasoning about Perception	using language to predict, reflect on, and integrate ideas and relationships	What will happen to the cookies when we put them in the oven?

Now we'll need a bowl to mix all these things together.
What shape is the bowl?
Oh, look how they are spreading out!
Let's think of some other things that we can bake in the oven.

In the next level of abstraction, *Reordering Perception,* the demands on the child are:

Tell me what we put in the bowl before we added the egg.
Show me the part of the egg that we don't eat.

At the fourth level of abstraction, *Reasoning about Perception,* the child is asked to theorize, explain, and rationalize. Continuing the illustration of the cookies, formulations at this level are:

Why don't we eat that part?
What will happen to the cookies when we put them in the oven?
We'll need to use a potholder because otherwise we'll burn our hands.

Table 2-1 highlights the relationship that exists between the scale of abstraction and the teacher's verbal formulations in our hypothetical lesson. That the examples can fit into the scale does not, by itself, prove the validity or worth of the model. It does, however, offer support for the usefulness of this approach in systematizing the wide range of language formulations that occur in the preschool setting.

The Other Components of Discourse

Until this point, we have devoted our efforts to elaborating on the component of discourse termed the "level of the discussion." As noted earlier, there are two other components in any interchange—the *speaker–listener dyad* and the *topic* or *subject* that they are discussing. In completing the presentation of our model, we will discuss briefly the role that these two other components play in the teacher–child exchange at the preschool level.

In considering these two components, it is important to keep in mind that they do not play the same role with younger children that they do with older students. For older children, high levels of complexity are both feasible and desirable in all three components. For younger children, though, simultaneous manipulation of three complex components is neither feasible nor desirable. The most that a young child can deal with is complexity in one component. Since programs have been constructed on the assumption that teachers ought to ask a range of relatively demanding and stimulating questions, we have designed our model so that there is complexity in the component that reflects these requests (the level of the discussion). The remaining components are held to a simple level. In this way, we hope to take account both of the child's limitations and the constraints of the preschool. Even though they are simple, these components represent important elements in any discussion.

First let us consider the issue of the speaker–listener dyad. In the case of older children, it is possible to lead students to abstract information for a great variety of both present and prospective listeners. Thus, students of high-school age could reasonably be asked to create a speech for their peers (i.e., students who are with them in the classroom), write an article for an audience they have never seen (e.g., readers of *Time* magazine), or prepare a talk for an audience that does not even exist (e.g., men from Mars).

In the case of the preschool setting, such wide variations among listeners almost never exist, nor, given the children's developmental limitations, could they be meaningfully imposed on them. We do not mean that young children will be unaware of the persons to whom they are speaking or that they will fail to modify their messages accordingly. (See Allen, 1973, Bloom et al., 1976; Garvey, 1977; Mueller, 1972; Schatz & Gelman, 1973 for illustrations of young children's effective and appropriate verbalizations.) Rather, we are saying that it is inappropriate to request that young children abstract their messages for a series of hypothetical prospective listeners. Accordingly, consonant with the actual preschool situation in which the teacher and child are in face-to-face contact, we have restricted the speaker–listener component in our model of discourse to these two persons. (There are, of course, also important exchanges among children themselves. Our interests, however, are focused on the verbal encounters between the teacher and the child that may lead to higher level intellectual activity in the child. Therefore, we have not concentrated our analysis on the peer component in the school setting.)

Just as the speaker–listener dyad can be highly variable with the older student, so too can there be great latitude in the topics available for discussion. Any idea—whether from the realm of history, morals, politics, economics, or science—represents a legitimate source for discussion. Such a limitless world does not hold for young children. A discussion about a presidential election, for example, would cover concepts that young children cannot grasp and generalizations that they could neither formulate nor understand. In addition, the short attention span of young children would almost certainly not permit them to carry out any sustained analysis such as that required by this sort of topic. Instead, the topics that might be discussed with young children are confined to activities that they can perceive and comprehend. Within this limitation, however, the variability ought to be as great as possible because variability serves both to maintain the children's interest and to lead them to generalize their use of discourse skills. Essentially, almost any activity that goes on in most preschool programs is a legitimate topic for discussion. These include class trips, stories, games, and activities with the teacher, such as cooking and gardening. Despite this variability, the topic component, like the speaker–listener component, represents a relatively simple factor in the model of discourse for a young child.

Table 2-2 is included here in an effort to indicate how the various components of discourse relate to each other. It is designed to show that two components (the speaker–listener dyad and the topic) are kept to simple levels while the third component (the level of the discussion) maintains considerable complexity.

We believe that the model captures essential elements of the demands that teachers put to children in their efforts to foster intellectual activity. As we have tried to indicate in our analysis, the demands proceed from simple

Table 2-2   *A Model of Discourse for the Preschool Age Child*

Component*	Constituents
1. speaker–listener dyad	teacher ⟷ child
2. topic of discussion	perceptually based experiences that are within the young child's level of comprehension
3. level of discussion	I Matching Perception
	II Selective Analysis of Perception
	III Reordering Perception
	IV Reasoning about Perception

*These categories have been adopted from Moffett's model (1968), as described in the preceding text, but represent the modifications that we have introduced to make the model appropriate for use with the preschool age range.

to relatively complex levels. This is the unavoidable, although generally neglected consequence of the ambitious goals that have been set. Activities such as reasoning, inference, and problem solving by definition require that the teacher impose complex and difficult tasks.

The posing of these demands is one matter; the children's ability to answer them is quite another. Given the documented limitations of young children, it may be that many of these demands are beyond their grasp. If so, the aims and the organization of the preschool curriculum would have to be altered considerably. Unlike the demands themselves, the children's ability to meet the demands cannot be studied through model building but only through a systematic assessment of the children's responses to the demands that are placed upon them. The development of an appropriate assessment instrument accordingly serves as the focus of the next chapter.

SUMMARY

Although language is the essential medium of exchange in classrooms, there is little systematic information on which facets of language are essential if the child's intellectual activity is to be stimulated by the instructional process. In an effort to deal with this problem, we have chosen a model developed by James Moffett and adapted it for use with the preschool-age child. In this model, classroom language is seen as a system of discourse involving three major components: the speaker–listener dyad, the topic, and the level of discussion.

For the preschool-age child, the model has been modified so the speaker–listener relationship is confined to the teacher–child interaction, and the topics discussed are confined to perceptually based experiences that the young child can comprehend. Within this framework the discussion can proceed along different levels of complexity. The dimension that unifies the different levels is the degree of separation that exists between the perceptual material available to the child and the language formulations that the teacher uses to lead him or her to analyze that material. The key points in this dimension are represented by the following phrases: *Matching Perception, Selective Analysis of Perception, Reordering Perception,* and *Reasoning about Perception.* This analysis of language will serve as the basis for the development of a test through which we can assess the preschooler's ability to cope with the demands of a verbally based instructional process.

3

A Test of the Preschooler's Discourse Skills

Central to our model of discourse is the idea that classroom language represents a dialogue situation that involves both teacher and child. While both participants are essential in the dialogue, their roles are not symmetrical. As in other settings, both teacher and child have a distinctive part to play. Given the goals of education, the teacher has the responsibility for presenting ideas and demands that lead the children to exercise their thinking and extend their cognitive mastery. The child, on the other hand, has the task of dealing with these ideas and demands (Bellack et al., 1966). These dual roles are reflected in the design of the test in which the range of demands represents the teacher's role (described in the first half of this chapter) and the types of responses represent the role of the child (described in the second half of this chapter).

THE DEMANDS MADE OF THE PRESCHOOLER

The language that a teacher uses covers both statements and questions. For example, a teacher may point out a feature of a car to the child by saying, "A car has four wheels." Alternatively, he or she may bring up the same idea by asking the child how many wheels a car has. While the child is expected to deal with both types of language, it is important to recognize that they do not lend themselves equally to assessment. Specifically, it is difficult to determine the child's comprehension of statements, for a statement by itself does not imply that the listener need offer any response. The child could appropriately remain silent with the result that one would have no knowledge as to how well she or he understood what was said.

In order to overcome this barrier, it becomes necessary to pose questions about the statements that have been offered; for example, after saying that a car has four wheels, one is likely to ensure a response by asking, "How many wheels did I say a car had?" Once this question has been asked, however, the child is no longer faced solely with a statement. Instead, he or she is faced with a question about a statement. As a result, should the child fail to answer appropriately, one cannot know whether the failure has been caused by difficulties in comprehending the original statement or by difficulties in answering the question about that statement or both. Because the comprehension of statements cannot be tested without the posing of questions or commands, it is impossible, within the confines of current techniques, to assess accurately the child's grasp of statements made by the teacher.

In contrast, questions and requests are not marked by these difficulties. By their very nature, questions and requests imply that the listeners are to offer a response. The skill that characterizes children's responses can be taken as a relatively direct measure of their ability to deal with the type of problem that has been posed. This aspect of the teacher's language therefore lends itself more readily to assessment. Accordingly, the teacher's role in the test of discourse has been confined to the demands that he or she may place on the children.[1]

As we have indicated in our model of discourse, the demands that teachers place on children range across a continuum of abstraction. At each level of the continuum, however, varied and extensive exchanges can take place. The example of the cookie-making lesson in Chapter 2 represents only a small sampling of the demands that a teacher can put to a child. In designing a test, it seems essential to sample as broad an array of these demands as possible. We have attempted to achieve this goal by constructing a comprehensive test with a large number of items at each level of abstraction. Thus, 34 items have been developed to assess level I demands, 37 items to assess level II demands, 51 items to assess level III demands, and 43 items to assess level IV demands. The total test, then, is composed of 165 items. The test is not designed to sample all of the demands that can be put to the young child. The great variety of content that may be discussed in any classroom exchange by itself precludes any such analysis (e.g., a discussion on number concepts may well have ques-

---

[1]We recognize that some readers may object to our limiting the analysis of classroom dialogue to the child's ability to cope with demands imposed by the teaching adult. This focus precludes any assessment of the child's cognitive-linguistic skills in other areas (e.g., in his or her spontaneous language with the teacher). But as noted earlier, we are interested in the degree to which the child can cope with and benefit from verbal formulations put forth by the teacher. It is for this reason that we have concentrated on this aspect of classroom language.

tions formed in a somewhat different way and certainly with a different set of concepts than will a discussion about a trip to the fire station). However, the test is designed to sample a relatively broad array of the major forms of demands that may be placed on the child at each level of abstraction.

In all cases, the items are designed to avoid laboratory tasks, that is, tasks which the child encounters only in highly contrived and artificial circumstances. Such tasks can be useful in identifying those children who will succeed and those who will fail. For example, a test such as finger tapping (e.g., counting how many times a child can tap his or her finger in a period of one minute) can be helpful in identifying those kindergarten children who will later have difficulty in reading (Satz & Sparrow, 1970). But tests like this one do not pinpoint the specific aspects of the school situation that are responsible for the child's difficulty. In other words, these tests help to reveal who will fail but they do not indicate what aspects of the actual school demands children can deal with effectively and which ones cause difficulty for them. It is precisely in this latter area that our interest lies. Accordingly, we have tried to construct all the items so as to mirror the language demands that are necessary in sustained teacher–child dialogue.

Our focus on discourse reflects itself in other aspects of the test design as well. Specifically, we are concerned with assessing the children's ability to follow, analyze, and report on ideas that are discussed in the classroom. If the ideas happen to contain references that are unfamiliar to the children, they will perform poorly—not because they lack discourse skills, but because they lack familiarity with the particular material. In order to minimize this possibility, the items have been designed to involve materials that are familiar to almost all children. In many cases, the items involve objects that are similar or even identical to objects that are present in the preschools which the children attend (e.g., they include materials such as toy cars, spoons, and crayons). The desire to minimize differences in familiarity has also led us to avoid questions that simply test the child's fund of knowledge or facts. Hence, we do not ask questions aimed at determining whether the child "knows colors" or "the parts of the body." Instead, wherever possible, the items are designed so that all the necessary information is made available to the children, and it is the children's task to apply their discourse skills to this information.

Just as certain types of items are excluded as being irrelevant to the process of discourse, so too are certain items included precisely because they are deemed to be central to this process. The items to which we are referring can be seen most clearly in the level III and IV demands, that is, Reordering Perception and Reasoning about Perception. (In the test, they are referred to respectively as Group III and Group IV demands.) Some characteristic items from these levels are, "how did you know that . . . would happen?" and "why did you choose . . . ?" Young children have not been extensively tested on these sorts of items for a number of reasons. For example, Piaget's interpretation (1951) of the preschooler's limitations has led many to think that such questions are beyond the young child's capability. There is, however, a growing controversy about the hypothesized limitations of the young child. In addition, as we have indicated in our model of discourse, we believe that demands of the third and fourth levels of abstraction are essential both to the full range of discourse and to adequate school performance. Accordingly, these types of demands occupy a central role in the test.

In order to illustrate the test most efficiently, it seems useful to present an outline of the actual demands that have been developed. The demands outlined subsequently are not meant to represent "hard and fast" categories. Rather, they are intended to offer a wide sampling of the vast range of demands that exists in the realm of discourse, even at the preschool age. The demands are grouped according to the four-level continuum of abstraction described in the preceding chapter. For each level there is a short statement highlighting the essential core of its demands. Following this, there is a brief outline of three of the items devised for testing a child's skill in this area. A description of all the test items is not offered in this chapter since it would require a lengthy description that would interfere with the flow of the text. For those who are interested, however, a description of the total array of items is presented in Appendix A. With these comments serving as a background, we will now present the four major groupings of test items.

Level I: Matching Perception

This category represents those language demands in which the child basically has only to respond to or report on salient perceptual information, that is, to apply language to information that ordinarily captures his or her attention. Many familiar demands made by teachers fall into this realm; for example, "what is this," "find one like this," "what things did you see," "what things did you hear," and "show me what you touched." Demands in this area typically involve short statements, commands, or questions by the teacher. In addition, nonverbal responses (e.g., pointing) or single-word responses from the child are often sufficient to meet the demand that has been posed.

The test items that have been developed for this group are intended to capture these qualities. The following represent three sample items.

Sample Item 1: Scanning for a Matching Object
Material   consists of an actual paring knife, and a large oaktag card containing 20 colored drawings of common objects. One of the drawings is like the knife; in addition, several of the items pictured are similar in shape or function to the knife (e.g., scissors), and some are associated with the context in which the knife is used (e.g., meat).
Task   the tester holds up the knife and says, "Look at this. When I show you the card, I want you to point to one like it." The tester then removes the knife from view and places the card in front of the child and says, "Now point to it."
Sample Item 2: Imitating a Simple Sentence
Material   none.
Task   the tester says, "You say what I say: *The ball was in the house.* "
Sample Item 3: Naming an Object Seen
Material   consists of a small, blue toy car.
Task   the tester shows the car to the child and asks, "What is this called?"

As indicated previously, these items are not intended to test the child's fund of knowledge (i.e., in asking, "what is this called," we are not interested in determining how many objects the child can name). Rather, we are interested in determining whether children know the types of information demanded by different questions and whether they can mobilize their knowledge to provide the information that is appropriate to the request. The label accompanying each demand (e.g., Scanning for a Matching Object, Imitating a Simple Sentence, and so forth) is intended to reflect this goal, for the label is an attempt to capture the dialogue process being assessed. The labels are not meant to be taken in an overly literal way. Rather, they are designed to highlight the range of demands that exists at each level of abstraction and to enable us to talk about these demands more easily.

At the level of Matching Perception, a total of nine processes are assessed, with each process being tapped by three to five items (e.g., the process of Naming an Object Seen is tested by asking the child to name a *car,* a pair of *scissors,* and a *cup*).The titles for each of the processes are listed here. As the reader will note, there is a brief parenthetical phrase following the title of each process. These phrases are designed to reflect the words that teachers typically use when placing this sort of demand on children. Specifically, the processes of group I are:

A. Scanning for a Matching Object *(Find one like this).*
B. Identifying an Object by Sound *(Show me what you heard).*
C. Identifying an Object by Touch *(Show me what you touched).*
D. Naming an Object Heard *(What did you hear?)*

E. Naming an Object Touched *(What did you touch?)*
F. Naming an Object Seen *(What is this ?)*
G. Imitating a Simple Sentence *(Say this. . . .)*
H. Remembering Pictured Objects *(What did you see?)*
I. Remembering Incidental Information *(What did you see?)*

As this list indicates, questions about the past as well as the present are included in Group I demands. It may be somewhat surprising to see, under the rubric Matching Perception, demands in which the material (i.e., the perception) is no longer available to the child. The perceptual-language distance continuum underlying the scale of abstraction, however, is focused primarily on the degree of correspondence between the perception (being discussed) and language (through which it is discussed). It makes relatively little difference if the perception is still available to the child at the moment that the question is asked. Indeed, in some cases the absence of the material can even be found to ease the communication task for young children.

This point can best be exemplified through an experimental task that was carried out with 3-year-olds (Blank, 1975). Initially, each child was required to learn to select consistently one of two shapes; for example, the child was shown a triangle and a circle. Then every time he or she chose the triangle rather than the circle, a candy was given. After each child solved the problem (as indicated by choosing the "correct" object in ten consecutive trials), he or she was asked to report which of the shapes was the "right" one. This demand is of interest here, for it was made in one of two contexts. In both contexts, the examiner said, "Tell me which one had the candy". In one context, however, the demand was put to the child while the objects were still in view, while in the other it was asked after the objects had been removed. Interestingly, the children were found to talk more readily about the materials when the objects were out of view rather than when they remained in sight. It appeared that when the materials were present, the children were not only more likely to gesture and point rather than verbalize (e.g., they pointed to the one that they had learned was "right"), but they were also more apt to be distracted by the physical appeal of something to manipulate. If the materials were absent, however, gestures such as pointing were rendered useless. The children then resorted to their verbal system (e.g., they said,"The triangle").

This example is not thought to be representative of all tasks involving present versus past. There are many times when a task involving the past will be more complex for the young child than will one involving the present. The complexity, however, will rest with the perceptual-language distance underlying the demand and it will not depend on whether the material under discussion is available to the child at the moment that it is being talked about.

Because language is so versatile, the demands within a single level of abstraction have been designed to differ in form and content. Furthermore, they can vary greatly according to the difficulty that they pose for the child. For example, it is generally harder for a child to identify an object by sound than by sight. In addition, even within a single process, the demands can be differentially difficult according to the particular materials that are used. Thus, it is easier for a child to follow the direction to find a particular object when the object is in an array of 5 or 6 items as contrasted to its being in an array of 15 to 20 items. Nevertheless, all of these demands are placed together within the first level of abstraction, Matching Perception, because they share the essential feature of that level; that is, they do not require children to move beyond the dominant perception that they are experiencing or have just experienced. These considerations (that is, that the items vary in difficulty but share an essential core of abstraction) apply as well to the remaining three groups of discourse demands.

Level II: Selective Analysis of Perception

This group, like the first, represents demands in which the children can continue to attend solely to the material before them. In this category, however, the demands require the children to focus more selectively on the material. Typically, these demands are reflected in the following phrases: *find something that we can use to . . .* , *name something that is . . .* and *who did . . . .* In addition, in this category, as well, are the familiar questions about the characteristics of objects that are heard in many classrooms (e.g., questions such as *what color is this, what shape is it,* and *how big is it*).

The demands in Group II are assessed through items such as the following.

1: Describing a Scene
Material   consists of a picture of a girl playing with a doll at a table set for tea.
Task   the picture is shown and the tester asks, "What's happening in the picture now?"
2: Recalling Information from a Statement
Material none.
Task   the tester says, "I'm going to tell you part of a story. The story starts like this: 'James and Ann walked down the street to see their friend's new car'." The tester then asks:

        a. What were the children's names?
        b. Where were they walking?
        c. What were they going to see?

3: Concepts; Identifying Differences
Material consists of a board with an actual scissors and knife.
Task the tester says, "Look at these. How are they different?"

The items in this category cover nine different processes. Again, they are fully described in Appendix A. The titles of the Group II processes and the key phrases through which the demands are imposed are as follows:

A. Scanning for an Object Defined by Its Function *(Find one that can . . . .)*
B. Describing a Scene *(What is happening?)*
C. Recalling Items Named in a Statement *(What things . . . ?)*
D. Recalling Information from a Statement *(Who? What? Where?)*
E. Completing a Sentence *(Finish this . . . .)*
F. Concepts: Naming Characteristics and Functions of Objects *(Tell me its . . . .)*
G. Concepts: Attending to Two Characteristics *(Find the one that is . . .and . . . .)*
H. Concepts: Identifying Differences *(How are these different?)*
I. Concepts: Citing an Example within a Category *(Name something that is a. . . .)*

Level III: Reordering Perception

The first two groups of demands reflect those tasks in which the children have to use language to describe or respond to experiences that they are currently perceiving or have just perceived. In the third category, the demands go far beyond this level as the children are required to evaluate material and ideas according to fairly subtle verbal constraints. As such, this category represents a major shift in the uses of language. Here, the language can no longer be mapped simply onto the children's perceptions; instead, their perceptions are reordered and restructured according to the language constraints that are imposed.

A typical demand in this category is the request for exclusion, that is, a demand in which the child must specifically exclude salient perceptual material. Linguistically, this demand is represented through terms such as *not, other than,* and *else.* The demand for exclusion is almost diametrically opposed to the young child's predisposition to be drawn to salient perceptual material (Zaporozhets & Elkonin, 1971). For example, suppose that there is a situation in which a child is shown a group of objects, most of them toys. Through their appeal and number, the toys not only represent a natural point of attraction, but also dominate the scene. Then imagine that the child is requested to, *give me all the things that are not toys.* Such a request is certainly appropriate in many settings, but its successful execution represents a major achievement for the child. First, it requires that the child reject the word that matches the perception, that is, the word "toys," and instead attend to the nonsalient but significant exclusion term, that is, the word "not." If the child fails to be directed by the negative and responds solely to the more focal noun (toys), it will be impossible for him or her to complete the task adequately.

A comparison of the verbal concepts of *same* and *different* may also help to reveal the critical dimensions that distinguish between demands at levels II and III. For example, let us suppose that a child is shown two *different* shoes—a woman's red sandal and a man's brown boot—and is asked, "How are they different?" An adequate response is possible in this situation if the child focuses on any number of dimensions (e.g., color, size, persons who wear them, and so forth) and then gives the relevant attributes from that dimension (e.g., *that's big, that's small; that's a lady's, that's a man's,* and so forth). As such, this demand requires a type of selective analysis similar to those of items in group II. The demand may not be easy, but it does not require young children to go beyond their perception (i.e., they are experiencing two things and must give a distinctive label to each). In contrast, with the identical materials, a different situation occurs when children are asked, "How are these the *same?*" Here, even though a single label, that is, shoe, could presumably meet the demand, that label does not represent the children's perception. Instead, their experience at the moment is of two different objects and, hence, it is not one of similarity but of difference. The children's predisposition, therefore, is to offer two different labels. In fact, many young children explicitly express this perception by replying, "They're not the same, they're different." For the demand to be met then, the children must overcome the dominant perception and think of a term that unifies the disparate impressions. This analysis of the situation leads us to place a demand for similarities in the third level of abstraction.[2]

The situations just discussed involve the presence of actual material. Also included in the group III category are demands for metalinguistic skills, that is, those demands in which the child must use language to talk about language, focus on language in unaccustomed ways, and play with language in what might be seen as early word games. These sorts of demands can serve an important role in classroom discourse and it has been speculated that their mastery may be vital to reading skill. (See Cazden, 1972, 1973a, 1973b; Gleitman & Rozin, 1973; and Liberman, 1973 for a more extended discussion of this topic.) As in the demand for exclusion, metalinguistic tasks require the child to inhibit strong, well-established responses and "rethink" the material to meet the request that has been

---

[2]Demands for verbally based concepts of similarity and difference should not be confused with perceptually based concepts of similarity and difference. For example, if a child is shown an object such as a ball and is asked to *find one like this,* there is no requirement for inhibition and reflection. Instead, the demand can be met by attending to salient features and then simply matching these features. As such, a demand for perceptual similarity represents a Group I demand.

imposed. For example, if a message is whispered to a child and he or she is asked to repeat it, the overwhelming urge is to whisper it in return. If, however, the request is made to repeat the whispered message in a loud voice, the child must repress the desire to whisper and instead simultaneously retain the content of the message while concentrating on the modifications that are necessary to meet the request.

Some sample items from Group III are as follows.

1: Assuming the Role of Another Person
Material   consists of a picture of a boy with one shoe off.
Task   the tester says, "A little boy came to school with only one shoe on." The tester then asks, "What did the other children say? What did the boy say?"

2: Formulating a Set of Directions
Material   consists of Lotto board and cards.
Task   after having matched the cards to the pictures on a Lotto board, the child is asked, "If you wanted to tell your friend how to play this game, what would you say to him (her)?"

3: Concepts: Citing an Example by Excluding a Class of Objects
Material   none.
Task   the tester says, "Listen, a lady was in the supermarket and saw something that was not food. What could she have seen?"

Fifteen processes are included in Group III and are outlined in Appendix A. The processes encompass the following demands:

A. Scanning for an Object by Integrating Verbal with Visual Information *(Find one to use with this.)*
B. Describing Events Subsequent to a Scene *(What will happen next?)*
C. Assuming the Role of Another Person *(What could he say?)*
D. Following a Set of Directions *(Do this, then this.)*
E. Arranging Pictures in a Sequence *(Make these into.)*
F. Formulating a Set of Directions *(Tell me how.)*
G. Formulating a Generalization about a Set of Events *(What* (same thing) *happened to all of these?)*
H. Formulating a Statement to Unify a Sequence of Pictures *(Tell this story.)*
I. Concepts: Identifying Similarities *(How are these the same?)*
J. Concepts: Selecting an Object by Exclusion *(What else . . . ?)*
K. Concepts: Selecting a Set of Objects by Exclusion *(Find the things that are not . . .)*
L. Concepts: Citing an Example by Excluding a Specific Object *(Name something that can . . . but is not a . . .)*
M. Concepts: Citing an Example by Excluding a Class of Objects *(Name something that is not a . . .).*
N. Concepts: Defining Words *(What is a . . . ?)*
O. Unusual Imitations *(Say this . . . .)*

Level IV: Reasoning about Perception

This category represents those complex verbal problems that require the child to reason about what may, might, could, or would happen to material under a stated set of conditions. On these tasks, the child must go beyond what he or she can perceive directly, and both discern the relationships among objects and events and formulate explicitly the reasons and logic responsible for these relationships. The problems involve demands such as:

1. predicting the effects of a proposed course of action (e.g., *what do you think will happen if . . .*)
2. identifying the causes for particular observations (e.g., *what do you think could have made the . . .*)
3. justifying the responses given (e.g., *why do you think that . . .*)
4. evaluating the essential and nonessential attributes of particular objects (e.g., *would it matter if . . .*)

In all these demands, the child must use the perceptual information accompanying the problem. In few cases, however, will a simple examination of the material reveal the information that is necessary for an appropriate response. For example, consider a problem in which the child is shown a boot and is asked, "Why are boots made of rubber and not paper?" Here, the perceptual information (provided by the boot) can be helpful, but at best it can serve only as a first step in meeting the problem. If this information is to be of use, the child must extract the specific features relevant to the problem. In this case, the child must inhibit his or her attraction to the total object and recognize that an attribute rather than the total object is relevant to meeting the problem posed. Then having made this decision, he or she must determine which of the many attributes of the boot is central in this specific instance; for example, he or she must determine if it is the boot's color, size, texture, or function that is important here. Further, *nothing in the organization of the perceptual material leads the child to recognize which attribute should be selected.* If anything, the more salient attributes—such as color—are irrelevant and therefore the child must learn to disregard them if he or she is to deal effectively with the problem. As this example shows, the language here goes far beyond a simple mapping of perception. Instead, the language is the vehicle for reflecting on and reasoning about perception. This aspect of discourse is deemed by many educators to be a vital part of effective teacher–child interchange. (See Bellack et al., 1966; Flanders, 1970; and Taba & Elkins, 1966 for work emphasizing this aspect of school language.) The following represent some sample demands that have been developed to assess this group of dialogue skills.

1: Predicting: Changes in Position

Material consists of a doll and a small box. The doll is facing the child, and the box is behind the doll.

Task the tester says, "If I turn the doll so that he is facing the box, what part of his head will you see?"

2: Justifying a Decision: Essential Characteristics

Material consists of two wooden semicircles and two wooden thin rectangular sticks.

Task the tester (referring to two semicircles) says, "I'm going to make a circle out of these." The tester proceeds to do so and says, "If I had used these [pointing to the straight sticks] instead of these [pointing to the other semicircles] to make this, would it still be a circle?" After child answers, tester asks the child, "Why?" or "Why not?"

3: Formulating a Solution

Material consists of 15 small items spread out on table; array includes a lollipop, a toy, a paper shopping bag, a sponge, and two balls.

Task the tester points to material and says, "If I wanted you to carry all these things over to that table, all at the same time, tell me what you could use."

A total of 14 processes are included to assess this group of skills. The titles and the key phrases representing these processes are:

A. Predicting: Changes in Position *(Where will . . . ?)*
B. Predicting: Changes in Structure *(What will happen if . . . ?)*
C. Justifying a Prediction *(Why will . . . ?)*
D. Justifying a Decision: Essential Characteristics *(Why wouldn't it . . . ?)*
E. Justifying a Decision: Nonessential Characteristics *(Why would it . . . ?)*
F. Identifying the Causes of an Event *(What made it happen?)*
G. Formulating a Solution *(What could you do?)*
H. Formulating a Solution from Another's Perspective *(What could she do?)*
I. Selecting the Means to a Goal *(What could we use?)*
J. Explaining the Means to a Goal *(Why should we use that?)*
K. Explaining the Construction of Objects *(Why is . . . made of that?)*
L. Explaining an Inference Drawn from an Observation *(How can we tell . . . ?)*
M. Explaining the Logic of Compound Words *(Why is this called . . . ?)*
N. Explaining the Obstacles to an Action *(Why can't we . . . ?)*

THE INTERWEAVING OF THE DEMANDS

Up to this point, the items under discussion have been presented in groups according to the level of abstraction that they represent. In the actual test, however, the items within any group are not presented together. Rather, the items from all four groupings are interwoven. This design may pose some difficulties for young children since it requires them to shift rapidly and flexibly among the demands as the test proceeds. But this requirement for shifting is one of the reasons why the test has been organized in this manner. A striking feature of naturally occurring dialogue is the great variability that it displays in content, structure, and complexity from one sentence to the next.

For example, in introducing a story to a group of children, a teacher might say:

> Children, I have a new book for you today. We haven't seen this book before, but we have met the little boy who is in it. Do you all remember when we read about Fred and the frog? Well, here's Fred again. This time, though, he's not with his frog. He's with somebody else. Here, look at the picture and tell me whom he's with this time.

In the first sentence of this hypothetical, but characteristic example, *I have a new book for you today,* the children are directed to a selected feature of the material, that is, a new book. The sentence thus represents a level II type demand. The second statement is designed to have the children attend not simply to the difference, but also to the similarity between this book and previously experienced books. It calls attention, too, to concepts of time (before) and exclusion (haven't seen). As such, this sentence touches on level III type demands. The remainder of the sequence shows a similar flow across the levels of abstraction and types of concepts.

For a variety of reasons, a test situation cannot mirror fully the pattern of natural discourse. For example, natural discourse stays, for at least a period of time, with the same theme. If a consistent theme were to be used in the test, it might be one that is unfamiliar to a child or group of children. As a result, they would perform poorly—not because of limited discourse ability, but rather because of the materials that happen to have been selected. To prevent this, a test must encompass a range of different materials so that no single material is of overriding importance. Similarly, natural discourse can flow in unpredictable directions, depending on the participants' interests and reactions. In the story presentation, for example, the teacher could easily have changed either the phrasing or the ideas if the children seemed unclear as to what was being said. An attempt to introduce this indeterminate quality to a test situation would destroy the possibility of systematic assessment. While the test situation has limitations, it nevertheless can be designed to capture some critical aspects of dialogue. The interweaving of the demands has been incorporated into the test for this purpose. In particular, it has been used to reflect the rapid shifting that is required if one is to be able to follow and contribute to any sustained discourse. (See Blank, 1973, for a fuller analysis of the characteristics of teacher–child dialogue.)

EVALUATING THE CHILD'S RESPONSE

Until this point, our focus has been on defining the demands of discourse that can occur in the classroom. As such, our analysis has been confined to only one side of the coin of formal discourse, namely, the requests that are imposed by the teaching adult. If we are to evaluate the children's skill in the dialogue, we must have some means of estimating the other side of the coin, namely, the children's ability to meet these requests.

As in any test situation, the problem arises as to how the children's ability is to be assessed. Generally, this problem has been handled by judging whether the responses that are offered do or do not meet the demands that have been imposed. In other words, the judgment becomes one of correct versus incorrect. (Occasionally the categorization is expanded to a three-tier system by introducing the grouping of part correct.) There are clear advantages to this type of categorization—it reduces the wide variability in behavior to manageable proportions, permits greater reliability and ease of scoring, and permits one to identify successful versus unsuccessful performance in whatever skill the test is measuring.

But accompanying these advantages is a weakness. As those familiar with young children know well, almost any question—whether in natural dialogue or in a test situation—yields an outstanding variety of answers. If asked, for example *what did you see at the zoo yesterday,* children may answer:

Animals and birds.
A tiger.
Popcorn.
Superman.
We didn't see any giraffes.
I don't remember.
A tree.
The Wicked Witch.
My brother is going to the circus.

If one chooses to remain solely with a correct–incorrect categorization, then, by necessity, different responses must be treated as equivalent. For instance, in the preceding illustration, responses such as *we didn't see any giraffes* and *Superman* are alike in that they fail to answer the demand that has been posed. Accordingly, they would both be treated as incorrect. Consequently, important distinctions between them are lost. For example, an answer such as *we didn't see any giraffes* indicates clearly that the child basically understands the topic under discussion and the response that he or she offers is geared to the question asked. In contrast, a response such as *Superman* shows no comparable understanding.

Table 3-1   *Assessment of Child's Response*

Sample task: Child is shown a toy balance scale containing weights on each side. The adult holds up a small weight and asks, "What will happen to the scale if I put another one here?" *(pointing to one side).*

Coding of Response	Score	Rule for Coding	Example of Response
Fully Adequate	3	Answer fully meets the demands of the task.	(pointing), "That side will go down."
Acceptable Imprecise	2	Answer is valid but is vague or poorly formulated.	(pointing), "Down."
Oblique		Answer is not directed to the focus of the problem.	"There'll be another thing in the cup."
Extraneous		Answer includes extraneous or irrelevant information.	"It will go down 'cos it's white."
Ambiguous	1	It is not possible to determine if answer is adequate or inadequate.	"It'll move."
Inadequate Invalid	0	Answer shows an understanding of the question, but the answer is incorrect.	"It will go up."
Association to Material		Answer indicates no understanding of the question, but it is focused on the material.	"It's red."
Irrelevant		a. Answer shows no understanding of the question or the material.	"I got one of those at home."
		b. Answer is an imitation of all or part of adult's words or actions.	"It will happen."
		c. Answer is a denial of the problem stated.	"You won't put it on."
I don't know*		Child states that he or she cannot answer.	"I don't know what'll happen."
No response*		Child offers no verbal response.	(shrugs)

*These two types of failure to respond are separated because clinically they seem to represent different behaviors. The verbalization *I don't know* is usually a sign that the child wishes to continue the exchange, whereas the nonverbal response is more indicative of a withdrawal from the dialogue.

Lack of understanding does not mean that the child's behavior is random. As Sigel (1975) has pointed out, "The error is the individual's expression of what he thinks is a right answer. Consequently, an error can provide some insight into the child's interpretation of the item" (p. 64). Therefore, if one fails to go beyond the categories of correct and incorrect, one loses the potential information that is available in the various types of incorrect responses that children offer. This loss of information is particularly crucial in a system that is designed to mirror the actual dialogue of the school. As we have emphasized, any dialogue yields a constant interaction between two participants. As a result, the child's response in the dialogue critically affects what the teacher will and should do next. In the illustration previously cited, for example, a response such as *Superman* could be seen in many ways to be similar to the response of *the Wicked Witch*. Both fail to speak to the question that has been asked, both bring in fantasy-like creatures, and so on. Accordingly, both might elicit similar responses on the part of the teacher.

In an effort to systematize the vast array of responses that children offer, it seems useful to turn once more to the concept of formal discourse. As stated earlier, central to this concept is the idea that the children are in a situation where they must abstract and communicate information about a topic. Accordingly, in assessing the child's answer, the yardstick that we have selected is the degree to which the response reflects the child's grasp of the demand that has been posed. This notion is reflected in a 10-point scale that proceeds from Fully Adequate responses to responses of increasingly less adequacy. In order to illustrate the scale, a sample problem, along with the coding for each type of response, is shown in Table 3-1.

The use of a term such as Fully Adequate in judging the children's responses does not mean that a single, prescribed response is necessary or desirable. With most discourse demands, any number of responses can be offered and can be judged as Fully Adequate. For example, consider the

---

Note: This scale applies to the majority of items in the test. In addition, a somewhat simpler scale is available for multiple-choice type items, that is, those items in which several objects are shown and the child has to select one object according to the problem posed. For example, the child is shown five different toy cars and is asked to find *the one that has a stripe and no top.* On these items, the child either chooses correctly (so that his or her response is Fully Adequate), or chooses incorrectly (so that his or her response is Inadequate). To reflect this, the Acceptable category is eliminated from the scale. In addition, on this type of task, it is not possible to discern differences among the various types of inadequate responses (i.e., the child simply chooses one of the other objects, but they are all equally inappropriate). As a result, the subcategories of Inadequate do not represent responses of different quality (as they do here) but simply reflect the particular item chosen by the child.

problem: "I saw a man this morning whose car was broken and he took it to the garage. What do you think he said to the garageman?" Here, the children can offer a huge variety of answers, all of which are adequate (e.g., *my car is broken, please fix my car, can you help me,* and *here's my car* all represent relevant, possible statements that a person in the hypothetical predicament could reasonably offer). The presence of a wide array of Adequate responses does not mean, however, that all responses can be viewed as appropriate. For example, *my daddy's car is broken* (which is not a statement that the hypothetical man would make), or *the man has to fix his car* (which shows a recognition of part of the problem, but fails to meet the demand that a quotation be offered) are types of answers that have failed to grapple with the essential demand. As such, they can be seen to illustrate various levels of Inadequate responses.

In evaluating the responses, it is important to keep in mind that the structure, complexity, or length of the child's response is not the central issue. Rather, it is the appropriateness of the response relative to the demand. In many cases, a pointing gesture can be fully sufficient. For example, in one problem the child is shown several intact paper stars along with a star that has had one of its points removed. The tester points to the intact stars and says, "I want to change these stars so that they look like this one," and the tester points to the atypical star. The tester then produces an array of objects and says, "Which one of these things can I use?" One of the objects in the array is a pair of scissors. If the child points to that object, the response shows that he or she has met the demands of the task, and therefore it is coded as Fully Adequate even though not a word has been said.

The advantage of this coding scheme is that the responses to each item in the test can be evaluated according to the same criteria. Appendix B offers examples of how the evaluations are made. It presents the coding that has been developed for each sample item outlined in Appendix A. With this coding system, it becomes possible to conduct a qualitative analysis of the responses that children offer to the total range of discourse demands. (Do some children consistently show high levels of Irrelevant responses? Do others show high levels of I Don't Know responses? and so forth) This analysis will play an important part in the evaluation of the results.

At the same time, however, we do not wish to lose the advantages accruing from the quantitative scores that are available with the more traditional correct–incorrect assessment. For this reason, we have chosen to apply a weighted score to the qualitative coding. Specifically, the scoring system is as follows:

a score of 3 for a Fully Adequate response
a score of 2 for an Acceptable response
a score of 1 for an Ambiguous response
a score of 0 for an Inadequate response

These numbers are listed in the second column of Table 3-1 next to the level of the response that they represent.

AN ILLUSTRATION OF THE TEST

Until now our comments have been directed toward giving the reader an overview of the test. Since a number of varied ideas have been covered, it may be easiest to integrate them by illustrating the administration of the test to a single child. This information is not designed to represent a "typical" child's performance, for no single child can represent the total group of preschool children. Rather, the information on this child is presented as a means of highlighting both the discourse demands that are included in the test and the range of responses that can be offered to these demands.

The child whom we have selected for this purpose is Adam, a boy age five years, five months, who comes from a middle-class environment. He is the elder of two children; the other child is a girl, age two. The parents are of different racial backgrounds—the father is white and the mother is black. Both parents are professionals; the father is a psychologist and the mother is a teacher. At the time of the testing, Adam was attending kindergarten in a private suburban school. Prior to this experience he had attended a Montessori nursery school for two years. His IQ as measured on the Stanford-Binet was 124.

With this information serving as background, we would now like to present Adam's performance on the test.[3] As noted above, in the actual testing the items within any group are not presented together. For ease of presentation, however, we have chosen to present Adam's performance on each group of items separately; that is, his performance on Group I, Group II, Group III, and Group IV are shown respectively in Figures 3-1 through 3-8, which are presented at the end of the chapter. The format for presenting each group of items is the same. The lefthand page presents the coding of the responses that Adam offered to that group of demands. It is designed to offer an overview of his performance on each of the four groups of items. For instance, in Group I the first process cited is Scanning for a

---

[3]Because of its length, the test is administered over a series of four sessions. The actual administration of the test will be discussed in Chapter 4.

Matching Object. That is, Adam was asked to select, from among an array of pictures, an object similar to one that he had just seen. The typical phrasing here is *find one like this.* Four items are administered to test this process. On these four items, Adam offers Fully Adequate responses to two of the items and Inadequate responses to the other two. One of the Inadequate responses consists of his saying *"I don't know";* in the other, he did not offer a response. His responses to each process are recorded in this way.

A summary of his performance to the total number of items in that group is shown on the bottom line. On Group I, for example, Adam offers 23 Fully Adequate responses, 5 Acceptable responses, and 6 Inadequate responses. The 23 Fully Adequate responses each receive a weighted score of 3, the 5 Acceptable responses a weighted score of 2, and the 6 Inadequate responses a weighted score of 0. (Had there been any Ambiguous responses, they would have received a weighted score of 1.) Accordingly, the mean for Adam's weighted scores on Group I is 2.3.

The righthand page is designed to offer specific illustrations of the demands posed and the responses offered. For this purpose, the sample item from each process is outlined. (These are the items that are described fully in Appendixes A and B.) For example, in Figure 3-2, in Scanning for a Matching Object, the sample item consists of the tester showing a paring knife and asking Adam, *find one like this* from a page containing the drawings of 20 common objects. As the chart indicates, Adam correctly fulfills the demands of the task. The remainder of the sample items and the responses they elicit are shown for each process in the group.

Thus far we have been discussing only the figures displaying the Group I demands and responses. The same considerations hold for the figures displaying the Groups II, III, and IV processes. By scanning across the four sets of charts, one can gain an overview of Adam's skill across the range of discourse demands. For example, his average score on Groups I, II, III, and IV, respectively, was 2.3, 2.6, 2.4, and 2.2. Given the weighted scoring system that has been established, the highest possible score is 3 and the lowest is 0. Adam's consistent attainment of scores above 2 indicates a high level of performance in all areas of discourse. Indeed, he offered Fully Adequate or Acceptable responses to over two-thirds of the items in every group. Because so many of his responses are in these categories, the number of Inadequate responses is naturally few. Nevertheless, by combining the types of Inadequate responses across the four groups, one can see some pattern begin to emerge. Specifically, they are distributed as follows: 5 Invalid, 6 Associated, 2 Irrelevant, 3 I Don't Know, and 1 No Response. These results indicate that the highest percentage of Adam's Inadequate responses are in the Invalid and Associated categories. These categories are notable in that while the child's response is not correct, it is nevertheless directed toward dealing with the problem that has been presented. In other words, in almost all instances, Adam is attempting to grapple with the demands even when he is unable to meet them.

SUMMARY

Our focus in this chapter has been on detailing the organization and content of a test that we have developed to assess the preschool child's skill in classroom discourse. The test is designed to mirror the roles played by both participants in the classroom, that is, to capture the roles of the teacher and the child.

The teacher's role is reflected in the various levels of demands that may be imposed on the child. Following the model presented in Chapter 2, four levels of demand are posited. For the first group of demands (Matching Perception), the language that the children must respond to and use essentially matches the salient perceptual features of the material before them; for example, they must give the name of an object that they see, such as a cup. For the next group (Selective Analysis of Perception), the children must begin to extract more selected features of the material; for example, they may be asked to recall information from a story. At the third level (Reordering Perception), the children must use language so as to restructure or reorder the way in which they view the material before them; for example, a picture may be shown of a boy riding a bicycle and the children may be asked, "What might the boy do after he finishes riding the bike?" The final level of abstraction (Reasoning about Perception) requires the children to deal with the realm of problem solving and reasoning; for example, they may be shown a paper cup with the bottom part missing and be asked to find the piece that could fill the opening. Then the children would be asked to give the reason why they chose the particular piece. The various levels of demands encompass 47 different processes and they are presented in 165 items. The total range of items is described in Appendix A.

The children's role in the dialogue is assessed through a scale that rates the quality of the response that they offer to each of the demands. The scale is distributed along a 10-point continuum that ranges from Fully Adequate responses to responses of increasingly lower degrees of adequacy. In addition to the qualitative analysis, a weighted score is also assigned to each response, as follows: 3 for Fully Adequate, 2 for Acceptable, 1 for Ambiguous and 0 for Inadequate. The weighted score permits one to offer a quantitative assessment of the child's performance in meeting discourse demands. The full scoring procedures for the range of demands are outlined in Appendix C.

	Coding of Responses									
Process	FA	Acc Imp	Acc Obl	Acc Ext	Amb	Inad Inv	Inad Ass	Inad Irr	Inad IDK	Inad NR
Weighted Score	3	2	2	2	1	0	0	0	0	0
A. scanning for a matching object — 4 items	●●								●	●
B. identifying an object by sound — 3 items	●●							●		
C. identifying an object by touch — 3 items	●●						●			
D. naming an object heard — 3 items	●●								●	
E. naming an object touched — 3 items	●●●									
F. naming an object seen — 3 items	●●●									
G. imitating a simple sentence — 6 items	●●●									
H. remembering pictured objects — 4 items	●	●	●●							
I. remembering incidental information — 5 items	●●	●	●						●	
total number in each category	23	2	3	0	0	0	1	1	3	1

Scoring

23 items received a score of 3 = 69
5 items received a score of 2 = 10
0 items received a score of 1 = 0
6 items received a score of 0 = 0
Total Weighted Score 79
Total Number of Items 34

Mean weighted score for Group I items = 2.3

Explanation of Abbreviations

FA — Fully adequate
Acc Imp — Acceptable—imprecise
Acc Obl — Acceptable—oblique
Acc Ext — Acceptable—extraneous
Amb — Ambiguous
Inad Inv — Inadequate—invalid
Inad Ass — Inadequate—associated
Inad Irr — Inadequate—irrelevant
Inad IDK — Inadequate—I don't know
Inad NR — Inadequate—no response

Figures 3-1 and 3-2 *Sample protocol for Group I demands: Matching Perception*

Sample Items			
Examiner's Demand	Child's Responses	Coded Response	Weighted Score
A. match a knife	selects knife	FA	3
B. select the item that made a sound	selects bell	FA	3
C. select the item that was held	selects ball	FA	3
D. name the thing that he heard	"bell"	FA	3
E. name the thing that he held	"ball"	FA	3
F. label a cup	"cup"	FA	3
G. imitate: the ball was in the house	"the ball was in the house"	FA	3
H. recall items in a picture	"carriage, coat"	Acc	2
I. recall objects that he had matched	"pencil, book"	Acc	2

	Coding of Responses									
Process	FA	Acc Imp	Acc Obl	Acc Ext	Amb	Inad Inv	Inad Ass	Inad Irr	Inad IDK	Inad NR
Weighted Score	3	2			1	0				
A. scanning for an object defined by its function 4 items	●●●			●						
B. describing a scene 2 items	●●									
C. recalling items named in a statement 2 items	●	●								
D. recalling information from a statement 6 items	●●● ●●					●				
E. completing a sentence 3 items	●●		●							
F. concepts: naming characteristics and functions of objects 9 items	●●●● ●●●	●●								
G. concepts: attending to two characteristics 3 items	●●●									
H. concepts: identifying differences 4 items		●●		●		●				
I. concepts: citing an example within a category 4 items	●●●●									
total number in each category	27	5	1	2	0	2	0	0	0	0
Mean weighted score for Group II items = 2.6										

Figures 3-3 and 3-4 *Sample protocol for Group II demands: Selective Analysis of Perception*

Sample Items			
Examiner's Demand	Child's Response	Coded Response	Weighted Score
A. find something to cut with	selects scissors and knife	FA	3
B. describe what is happening in a picture	"someone's pouring some tea"	FA	3
C. tells of a cat and a lady, asks child to recall them	"cat and lady"	FA	3
D. tells about James and Ann, asks child for their names	"Joan, and I forget"	Inad Inv	0
E. finish sentence: I like to eat some	"supper"	FA	3
F. tell: what do we do with a cup?	"drink out of it"	FA	3
G. shows four cups, asks which one is upside down with pictures	points correctly	FA	3
H. tell how a scissors and knife are different	"'cause these open" [scissors] and this doesn't [knife]"	Acc Imp	2
I. name something that has wheels	"bicycle"	FA	3

		Coding of Responses								
Process	FA	Acc Imp	Acc Obl	Acc Ext	Amb	Inad Inv	Inad Ass	Inad Irr	Inad IDK	Inad NR
Weighted Score	3	2			1	0				
A. integrating verbal with visual information 4 items	●●●●									
B. describing events subsequent to a scene 2 items	●				●					
C. assuming the role of another person 5 items	●●●	●			●					
D. following a set of directions 2 items	●●									
E. arranging pictures in a sequence 3 items	●●●									
F. formulating a set of directions 2 items		●●								
G. formulating a generalization 3 items		●		●	●					
H. formulating a statement to unify a sequence of pictures 2 items	●●									
I. concepts: identifying similarities 4 items	●		●			●		●		
J. concepts: selecting an object by exclusion 2 items	●●									
K. concepts: selecting a set of objects by exclusion 4 items	●●	●●								
L. concepts: citing an example by excluding a specific object 4 items	●●●						●			
M. concepts: citing an example by excluding a class of objects 4 items	●●●●									
N. concepts: defining words 3 items		●●●								
O. unusual imitations 7 items	●●●●	●●			●					
total number in each category	31	11	1	1	4	1	1	1	0	0

Mean weighted score for Group III items = 2.4

Figures 3-5 and 3-6 *Sample protocol for Group III demands: Reordering Perception*

Sample Items

Examiner's Demand	Child's Response	Coded Response	Weighted Score
A. shows orange and says, "find something to cut it with"	selects knife	FA	3
B. shows picture of a boy on a bike and says, "what might happen next?"	"put the bike away"	FA	3
C. asks what other children would say if a boy had one shoe on	"Why do you have one shoe on?"	FA	3
D. to take socks off doll, put hat in box, and put box on the floor	carries out all actions	FA	3
E. to arrange pictures of a boy eating an apple	places pictures in correct sequence	FA	3
F. to say what the child would say to another to explain lotto	"What's under here?"	Acc Imp	2
G. to tell what happens to water when dyes are put in	"they turned dark"	Acc Imp	2
H. to describe pictures of a glass being filled with water	"first it's empty, then there's a little water, then more water"	FA	3
I. to tell how scissors and knife are the same	"this one cuts things and this one cuts things"	FA	3
J. shows pencil, asks the child to find something different that writes	selects a pen	FA	3
K. to select from array all the things that are not dolls	selects rattle, ball, toy	FA	3
L. to name something that writes that is not a pencil	"magic marker"	FA	3
M. to name something in supermarket that is not food	"toys"	FA	3
N. to answer: *what is a cup?*	"you drink out of it"	Acc Imp	2
O. to repeat: *what does the dog say?*	"what does the dog say?"	FA	3

Coding of Responses

Process	FA	Acc Imp	Acc Obl	Acc Ext	Amb	Inad Inv	Inad Ass	Inad Irr	Inad IDK	In
Weighted Score	3	2	2	2	1	0	0	0	0	
A. predicting: changes in position　　2 items	●●									
B. predicting: changes in structure　　5 items	●●●		●	●						
C. justifying a prediction　　5 items	●	●●				●	●			
D. justifying a decision: essential characteristics　　2 items		●●								
E. justifying a decision: nonessential characteristics　　2 items	●●									
F. identifying the causes of an event　　2 items	●						●			
G. formulating a solution　　2 items	●					●				
H. formulating a solution from another's perspective　　1 item							●			
I. selecting the means to a goal　　4 items	●●●●									
J. explaining the means to a goal　　4 items	●	●●			●					
K. explaining the construction of objects　　3 items	●●	●								
L. explaining an inference drawn from an observation　　2 items	●●									
M. explaining the logic of compound words　　3 items	●●				●					
N. explaining obstacles to an action　　6 items	●●				●●●●					
total number in each category	23	7	1	2	5	2	3	0	0	●
Mean weighted score for Group IV items = 2.2										

Figures 3-7 and 3-8　*Sample protocol for Group IV demands: Reasoning about Percept*

Sample Items			
Examiner's Demand	Child's Response	Coded Response	Weighted Score
A. to tell what part of the doll's head would be seen if the doll were turned	"the back" (points)	FA	3
B. to tell what would happen to a pile of blocks if the bottom block is pulled out	"it will be just a little bit this way" (motions with hand)	Acc Obl	2
C. to justify answer (in B)	"because if you take this off, it will be a little bit"	Inad Ass	0
D. to say why a circle made of straight lines would not remain a circle	"it would only be a triangle"	Acc Imp	2
E. to say why a circle made out of blue, not red, paper would remain a circle	"'cause it would just be a a different color"	FA	3
F. to say how she or he made flashlight go off	"when I press this down, it goes off"	FA	3
G. to tell how to carry many items at one time	points to a shopping bag	FA	3
H. to say what a child could say to another who wanted a drink	"the sink is over here" (points)	Inad Ass	0
I. to find something to change stars to match a star missing one point	selects scissors	FA	3
J. to explain selection (in I)	"because you can cut with this, but you can't cut with these"	FA	3
K. to say why a key is made of metal, not cloth	"if you put this in [points to cloth] it would bend"	FA	3
L. to say how one could tell that a person looked happy	"'cause this one is smiling"	FA	3
M. to say why a buttonhole is called by that term	"'cause this is for a button"	Amb	1
N. to say why duplicate piece could not fit into completed puzzle	"'cause there's the head and this can't go in if it's the head"	Acc Imp	2

4

The Children and the Testing

SELECTING THE SAMPLE

We now turn our attention to a description of the children who received the test of discourse skills.[1] In selecting the children, we chose to be guided by the common practice of including as preschoolers children from age 3 to 5 years (i.e., 36 to 71 months). Because of the marked changes in performance that occur across this age span, it seemed essential to divide this 36-month period into smaller intervals and ensure that equal numbers of children were seen at each of these intervals. In order to accomplish this, the total period was divided into nine 4-month intervals (i.e., 36 to 39 months is one interval, 40 to 43 months is a second interval, and so on). Within each 4-month interval, 32 children were selected for testing. Hence, the total sample was composed of 288 children.

Selection of the age ranges, however, was not the only factor to be considered. As mentioned in Chapter 1, the preschool has been selected as a major vehicle for dealing with school failure in children from lower-class backgrounds. If the preschool is to execute this function, it is essential for it to have firm knowledge about the ability of these children to comprehend and participate in the teacher–child exchange. In an effort to gain this information, we chose to have children from lower-class backgrounds occupy a relatively large proportion of the sample. That is, we elected to divide our sample equally between preschool-age children from lower-class and middle-class backgrounds. Accordingly, half of the 32 children in each 4-month interval came from lower-class backgrounds

---

[1]The testing that is reported took place between September 1972 and February 1974.

Table 4-1   *Number of Children in the Sample According to Age, Sex, and Socioeconomic Status*

Age Range (in months)	Middle Class		Lower Class	
	Male	Female	Male	Female
36–39	9	7	7	9
40–43	9	7	8	8
44–47	8	8	5	11
48–51	5	10	6	11
52–55	11	6	8	7
56–59	8	8	8	8
60–63	8	8	8	7
64–67	8	8	8	9
68–71	8	8	8	8
Total	74	70	66	78

and half from middle-class backgrounds.[2] In addition, as far as was possible, we attempted to have relatively equal numbers of boys and girls in each 4-month interval. Table 4-1 provides an overview of the sample that was selected.

As is well known, numerous problems exist in the determination of social class. In practice, the terms *lower class* and *middle class* represent a composite of variables, based primarily on measures such as family income, educational level, and occupation rating. Rather than attempt to consider all these factors in the selection of the children, we chose to be guided solely by the school that the child attended. Specifically, the lower-class children were drawn from 13 day care centers located in poor (inner city) neighborhoods in New York City; the middle-class children were drawn from 11 private nursery schools in more affluent sections of the city and neighboring suburban areas.

Although school placement is only a single measure, the constellation of variables accompanying this measure allowed it to provide a sufficiently

---

[2]In other words, we chose *not* to select a sample that was representative of the population at large; that is, in a representative sample, the population studied would have mirrored the proportions of the total population from which it was drawn. Although representative sampling is commonly employed, it seemed inappropriate in the present circumstances. Given the distribution of the population in the United States, a representative sample would have contained no more than about 10 percent to 20 percent of children from lower-class backgrounds. Thus, a sample of 300 children would contain only about 30 to 60 such children. As a result, we would have obtained relatively little information on the way in which lower-class children function on the skills that we hoped to analyze.

complex basis for the assignment of social class. For example, children received a place in a day care program only after careful screening by the center officials on a variety of factors that usually determine social class (i.e., the family income had to be below a certain level, the family situation had to be such that the mother worked or was overburdened, and so forth). Similarly, the fees and hours of the private nursery schools meant that the families were of middle-class background (i.e., the families could afford the expense, the children were in school only a few hours and then returned home to their mothers who were not working or to housekeepers whom the families could afford, and so forth).

Our use of school placement was supported by background information that was obtained on all the children on a number of variables that correlate with social class. These included the parents' occupations, the absence of either parent from the home, the number of siblings, and the ethnic background of the children. These data will be discussed briefly to provide a fuller picture of the children in our sample.

Occupations of the Parents

Wherever possible, information was obtained on both the father's and mother's occupations. These were then ranked according to a modified scale that we adapted from the Hollingshead Occupational Index (Hollingshead & Redlich, 1958). The scale covered 12 categories:

  I. higher executives, proprietors of large concerns, and major professionals
 II. business managers, proprietors of medium-sized concerns, and lesser professionals
III. administrative personnel, small, independent business owners, and semi-professionals
 IV. occupations with a rating of at least 3 or higher; from the available information, however, it is not possible to determine the exact rating
  V. clerical workers, sales workers, technicians
 VI. skilled manual employees
VII. machine operators and semiskilled employees
VIII. unskilled employees
 IX. some employment but exact nature unknown
  X. paraprofessionals—in training for improved jobs
 XI. on welfare
XII. no information available

The distribution of the sample according to the occupational level of the parents and social class is shown in Table 4-2. In this table, the rating was

Table 4-2   *Distribution (percent) of the Families According to Occupational Level*

Occupational Rating*	Social Class Background	
	Middle	Lower
I	27	1
II	15	1
III	10	2
IV	11	1
V	10	30
VI	6	4
VII	1	12
VIII	0	4
IX	3	6
X	0	12
XI	0	8
XII (no information)	17	19

*Based on a modification of the Hollingshead Occupational Scale.

generally based on the father's occupation. That is, whenever information was available about the father, we used that information to categorize the family's occupational level. When information about the father's occupation was not available, however, we turned to the mother's occupation as a means of gaining some indication of the family's occupational status. Information on the father's occupation was available for 111 of the middle-class children and for 46 of the lower-class children. The use of the mother's occupation permitted us to classify an additional 9 middle-class children and 70 lower-class children. We were unable to obtain information on the occupation of either parent for 24 middle-class and 28 lower-class children.

As shown in Table 4-2, there was some degree of overlap between the occupational levels of the two groups.[3] In general, however, the sample did show the expected occupational differences in that well over the majority of children classified as middle-class had parents whose occupations were rated from I to IV, while the parents of children classified as lower-class had ratings that tended to fall in the categories of V and below.

---

[3] In some cases, there were also some unexpected placements in the occupational scale. For example, one boy from the day care center population came from a family with a rating of 1, as he was the child of a medical student. The father was in a minorities program at a medical school in the city and the mother was working in a community agency to support the family. Their preschool-age child was in the day care center in order to permit the mother to work.

Family Size and Birth Order

Because birth order has been shown to affect cognitive and school performance (Altus, 1966; Broman et al., 1975; Zajonc, 1976), it seemed useful to look at the relationship between family size and the birth order of the children. As shown in Table 4-3, there was a relatively small difference between the social classes in the average family size. Middle-class families averaged 2.2 children whereas lower-class families averaged 2.4 children. Among the lower-class, there was a strong trend for the families to be divided among one-, two-, and three-children families. Among the middle class, however, the majority (61 percent) came from families with two children (i.e., there were fewer one-child and three-children homes). All of the children from the one-child families were, of course, first born. In the present sample, this included 22 middle-class and 45 lower-class families. In addition, of the remaining children, 56 middle-class and 21 lower-class children were also first born. In other words, 78 middle-class children and 66 lower-class children were the first-born children in their families. This represented a fairly high percentage of the sample, specifically 54 percent of the middle-class and 46 percent of the lower-class groupings.

Intactness of the Families

In all cases, efforts were made to gain information about the presence of the father in the home. Although this goal was not attained in every case, information on the father's presence was available for 83 percent ($N = 120$) of the middle-class and 87 percent ($N = 125$) of the lower-class families. When we considered only those cases in which information was available, we found that the father was present in 94 percent ($N = 113$) of the middle-class homes and 35 percent ($N = 44$) of the lower-class homes. Among the middle-class families, in all cases in which the father was

Table 4-3   *Distribution of the Families According to the Number of Children*

Social Class		\multicolumn{5}{c}{Number of Children}				
		1	2	3	4	5+
Middle	N	22	84	19	10	3
	%	16	61	14	7	2
Lower	N	45	37	34	11	11
	%	33	27	24	8	8

N=number of families.

%=percent of the total sample within each social class.

known to be absent (*N* = 7 or 6 percent), the children lived with their mothers. Among the lower class families, 77 of the children (62 percent) lived with their mothers and 4 (3 percent) lived with neither parent but were cared for by other members of the family (grandparents, aunts, and so on).

Ethnic Background

The ethnic distribution of the lower-class children was as follows: 5 percent white, 77 percent black, 17 percent Puerto Rican, and 1 percent Asian. The ethnic distribution of the middle class was 86 percent white, 12 percent black, 1 percent Puerto Rican, and 1 percent Asian. The numbers that these percentages represented (within the total sample of 288 children) are shown in Table 4-4. As is clear from the figures there, class and race were confounded, with the black and Puerto Rican children coming predominantly from the lower class, and the white children coming predominantly from the middle class. Although it would have been desirable to have included a large white lower-class group and a large black middle-class group, the distribution of the population in the metropolitan area did not allow us easily to obtain these subgroups.

IQ Performance

Each child was also given an individual IQ test. The test used was the 1960 revision of the Stanford-Binet Intelligence Scales, Form L-M. The IQ test was administered in a session prior to the administration of the test of discourse skills and it was given by a person other than the one who was to later test the child on the discourse skills. The administration of the IQ test enabled us to eliminate from the sample those children who were retarded or unable to speak English. In addition, the IQ test enabled us to gain a picture of the children's general cognitive performance and thereby to

Table 4-4 *Distribution of the Children by Social Class Background, Ethnic Group, and Sex*

Social Class	Ethnic Group								
	White		Black		Puerto Rican		Asian		Total
	Male	Female	Male	Female	Male	Female	Male	Female	
Middle	65	59	9	9	0	1	0	1	144
Lower	5	3	49	61	12	12	0	2	144
Combined	70	62	58	70	12	13	0	3	288

analyze the degree to which the discourse skills were related to such performance. This analysis will be considered in the next chapter. In the interim, it seems useful to present the way in which the children's IQs were distributed.

IQ scores, grouped by age, sex, and socioeconomic status are presented in Table 4-5. The mean IQ of the middle-class sample was 121.6 with a standard deviation (SD) of 15.6; that of the lower-class sample was 102.1 with a standard deviation of 13.3. In addition, the IQ scores for middle-class females were approximately 2 to 4 points higher than their male counterparts at all three ages. This performance was consonant with previously reported findings (Broman, et al., 1975, p. 43). In the lower-class sample there was a sex difference in IQ scores only at age three, with the females obtaining IQ scores approximately 4.5 points higher than their male peers.

Overall, the IQs in this sample were higher than those generally reported in the literature. However, they were in line with recent reports on enhanced IQ performance among young children (Thorndike, 1976). In addition, the higher IQs might have resulted from other factors. For example, both groups of children came from families who had sought out early educational experiences for their children. Therefore, they might not have been representative of the general range of either the middle or lower class. Despite the general upgrading of IQ scores, our data nevertheless yielded an IQ difference between the social classes that is about the same magnitude as that previously reported (Dreger & Miller, 1960; Jensen,

Table 4-5   *IQ Distribution by Age, Sex, and Socioeconomic Status*

Age (in years)	Middle Class				Age (in years)	Lower Class			
	Sex	N	Mean	SD		Sex	N	Mean	SD
3	Male	26	121.3	17.1	3	Male	20	102.1	13.3
	Female	22	125.9	16.6		Female	28	106.6	10.2
	Combined	48	123.4	16.9		Combined	48	104.8	11.7
4	Male	24	119.1	15.5	4	Male	22	101.9	12.7
	Female	24	120.8	11.4		Female	26	102.3	12.7
	Combined	48	120.0	13.4		Combined	48	102.1	12.6
5	Male	24	119.5	17.9	5	Male	24	99.6	18.1
	Female	24	122.2	14.8		Female	24	99.0	11.7
	Combined	48	120.8	16.3		Combined	48	99.3	15.1
Total		144	121.6	15.6			144	102.1	13.3

1973; and Loehlin et al., 1975). The middle-class IQ scores tended to peak in the 112–117 range while the lower-class IQ scores tended to peak in the 100–105 range. This result is depicted in Figure 4-1.

THE FORMAT OF THE TESTING

Each child who was selected for the sample was tested individually in a room in his or her school. Since the test of discourse skills was extensive (it included 165 items), it was not possible to administer it within a single session. Instead, the test was divided into four parts, with each part being given on a separate day. Each part was comprised of items from the four groupings described in Chapter 3; that is, items from the various group- ings were interspersed with one another so that items from all four group- ings were present on each of the four days.

The adults who did the testing initially sat in with the children in each classroom for a minimum of three days so that the children could become well acquainted with them. Two adults were present at each testing ses- sion. One person administered the test items; the other recorded the chil- dren's responses. A total of eight women were involved in administering the testing. All were experienced in dealing with preschool age children. Each person served, at different times, in the role of tester and recorder.

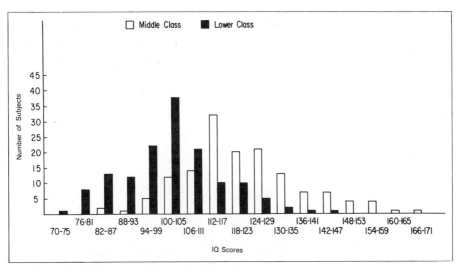

Figure 4-1   *IQ distribution of total sample by socioeconomic status.*

With any one child, however, consistency was maintained so that the same person was the tester and the other person was the recorder over the four sessions. In addition, four of the eight were trained to score the protocols that were obtained. The person who scored the protocol was always different from the person who administered the test.[4]

AN OVERVIEW OF THE SAMPLE AND THE TESTING

Since a number of different factors have been covered in this section, it seems useful at this point to highlight the essential features of the children with whom we worked and the format we used in our contacts with them. A total of 288 children were tested. They ranged in age from 36 to 71 months. Half the sample came from lower-class backgrounds; the other half came from middle-class backgrounds.

The assignment of social class background was made on the basis of school placement, with the lower-class children coming from day care centers and the middle-class children coming from private nursery schools. This measure correlated with variables that are commonly associated with differences in social class such as parental occupation and IQ performance. Within each social class, the children were divided approximately equally between boys and girls. As far as could be ascertained, all the children were in good health and displayed no severe problems in either the physical or emotional spheres.

Each child selected for the study was tested individually in a room in his or her school. The test of discourse was carried out over four days, with the testing on each day lasting about 20–25 minutes. Two adults were present at each session; one administered the test items, the other recorded the child's responses.

---

[4]Because of the complexity of the scoring system that was used, the issue of rater reliability was crucial, that is, the extent to which the raters agreed in their scoring. To determine this, all four raters independently scored the protocol of every tenth child in the sample. On each of the 28 protocols scored in this way, there was total agreement which ranged from 92 percent to 97 percent.

5

The Children's Performance

This chapter presents the findings obtained from the testing that was conducted. The analysis is geared to answering the following two questions:

1. Do preschool children possess the language skills that are needed for engaging in productive verbal exchange with teachers?
2. If they do possess such skills, to what extent are these skills equivalent in preschool-age children from middle- and lower-class backgrounds?

We will consider each of these questions in turn.

THE PRESCHOOLER'S MASTERY OF DISCOURSE

The phrasing of the first question contains an important, albeit implicit, premise. It indicates that our primary interest is not in comparing one child with another but rather in comparing all preschool children against a standard that reflects skill in discourse. This orientation directs this section of the analysis away from the commonly emphasized theme of individual differences (i.e., how different children perform on the test). Although such differences are bound to occur, they may be inconsequential in the school situation. For example, despite variations in scores, all of the children could be found to possess sufficient skill in discourse to function effectively in the classroom. Conversely, none might be found to function in this manner. These are not the only possible outcomes; the percentage of preschool-age children who possess adequate discourse skills could be found to vary anywhere from 0 percent to 100 percent. We have cited the extremes solely to highlight the fact that the key issue here is not the comparison of the children among themselves but rather the evaluation of their performance against an agreed-upon standard of achievement. Implementation of this strategy can be accomplished, however, only if there is an available criterion that defines the level of test performance deemed to reflect adequate skill in discourse.

The problem of establishing standards of achievement is similar to that in criterion-referenced testing in which the goal is to determine if a child has attained an acceptable level of accomplishment in a designated subject. (See Glaser, 1963, and Glaser & Nitko, 1971, for an extended discussion of these issues.) For example, before advancing a child into a higher level course, one might administer a criterion-referenced test to determine if the child had incorporated the material that had been offered thus far. A term that is commonly employed within this frame of reference is *mastery learning* (Bloom, 1973). It is designed to represent the idea that students can be assessed on whether or not they have mastered or achieved the skills in a particular sphere. Because of its relevance, we have chosen to adapt the concept of mastery to the realm of discourse. Specifically, we have chosen to use the 50 percent level of success—that is, the point at which a child achieves Adequate responses on half the items in any group—as the criterion for mastery of that level of abstraction.[1] This criterion has been selected because it represents the point at which the child's performance shifts from a predominance of Inadequate responses to a predominance of Adequate ones. The choice is arbitrary, and ultimately it may be found that a 60-percent or a 75-percent criterion is more suitable. Nevertheless, as a beginning formula the 50-percent criterion seems a reasonable place to start.

The initial evaluation of the children's performance is based on the criterion of mastery just outlined. Given the scoring system used for the test (3 for Fully Adequate, 2 for Acceptable, 1 for Ambiguous, and 0 for Inadequate), the highest mean score possible is 3 and the lowest is 0. With this scoring system, the 50 percent level occurs at a mean of about 1.5.

Figure 5-1 presents the percentage of three-, four-, and five-year-old children who have achieved scores of 1.5 or greater on each of the four groups of discourse skills. The four groups of skills have been evaluated separately since each is deemed to require different levels of abstraction. As occurs with almost any skill, there is a steady improvement in the children's performance with age (i.e., the four-year-olds achieve higher scores on all four groups of tasks than do the three-year-olds; the five-year-olds,

---

[1]In using the criterion of mastery in this way, it is clear that we are differentially attending to certain aspects of the concept. For example, mastery learning is assessed *after* the children have received instruction in some subject. Here, however, we are using it to reflect the degree to which the child has achieved the skills that we have deemed must exist *prior* to instruction. Although our use of the term is different from that used in the achievement testing area, the two uses of the term are similar with respect to the idea that children can be assessed on the adequacy with which they have learned to deal with a particular body of knowledge or skill.

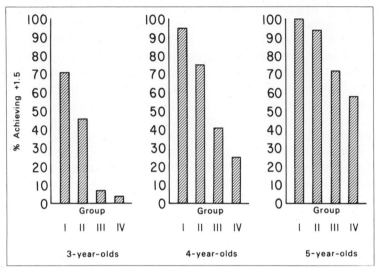

Figure 5-1   *Percentage of all children achieving above 1.5 criterion at each age.*

in turn, achieve higher scores than do the four-year-olds). In addition, the four groups of skills also progress in difficulty in the way anticipated in our model of discourse; that is, Group I tasks that require the least abstraction yield the highest scores, and the Group IV tasks that require the most abstraction yield the lowest scores. The scores for Groups II and III fall between these two extremes.

What is important for our purposes, however, is the high proficiency exhibited by the preschool children in the sphere of discourse. Even the three-year-olds evidence mastery of discourse skills, although admittedly their mastery tends to be confined to the Group I and Group II areas (i.e., 71 percent and 46 percent of the three-year-olds achieve the 1.5 criterion on Groups I and II, respectively). This is not to say that three-year-olds offer Acceptable responses to all Group I and II demands. Rather, the results suggest that they comprehend most Group I and II type exchanges. As we will demonstrate in the next chapter, this range of ability offers a sufficient base for creating and maintaining relatively rich exchanges between a teacher and a child. Demands at the Group III and IV levels, however, seem to be beyond the level of understanding of most three-year-olds (i.e., only 7 percent and 4 percent of this age range achieve the 1.5 level on Group III and IV demands respectively). By age five, the picture changes considerably in that a high percentage of children have achieved mastery over all four groups of discourse skills; that is, 100 percent achieve the 1.5 criterion on Group I skills, 94 percent on Group II, 72 percent on Group III, and

58 percent on Group IV. As noted in Chapter 4, our sample is not representative of the population in our country and a different set of percentages might well be obtained if a representative sample were tested. Nevertheless, the fact that well over half of the five-year-olds achieved the criterion of mastery on Group III and IV skills suggests that a high percentage of preschool age children can cope effectively with the total range of dialogue skills that may occur in classroom exchange.

The analysis thus far has been based on the 50 percent criterion of success. Lest such a criterion reflect too low a level of success, the children's performance has also been analyzed according to the 67 percent level; that is, the level at which the children offer Adequate responses to two-thirds of the demands put to them. In our scoring system, this level of performance coincides with a score of about 2. Figure 5-2 depicts the results that are found when the scores are considered according to this criterion. As can be seen there, 38 percent and 30 percent respectively, of the five-year-old children continue to achieve mastery on the Group III and IV skills even when this more stringent criterion is used. In other words, a sizeable percentage of five-year-olds evidence high levels of performance in the realm of formal discourse.

Their skill in this area can be seen through some actual responses that have been elicited in the testing. The following answers are ones that four- and five-year-old children offered to the rather intricate Group III and IV problems:

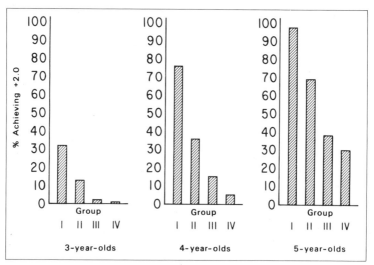

Figure 5-2   *Percentage of all children achieving above 2.0 criterion at each age.*

When asked if a circle made out of blue rather than red paper would still be a circle, one child replied "Yes, because it really doesn't matter what color it will be."

When asked what a man would say to a man in the garage if his car were broken, one child replied, "Please fix my car." When asked to shift his perspective and say what the man in the garage might reply, he offered the response, "I'll be glad to."

When asked, after seeing a red rod mixed in with others of the same color, why it was not possible to find the one that had been put in, one child replied, "Because there are some red ones, too, and they all look the same."

When asked what would happen if additional weights were added to a scale, one child replied, "It would go down this way, and if you added a lot, it would tip over."

When asked—after a box with marbles had been rattled before him— if the box would still make a noise if there were no marbles in it, one child replied, "No, because then only air is there, and air doesn't make a sound."

When asked why boots are made of rubber instead of paper, one child replied, "Paper can get ruined, rubber can't."

When asked if a sponge would still be a sponge if it were in the shape of a circle instead of a rectangle, one child replied, "Yes, because sponges could be all shapes."

When asked to describe "the story" in a set of pictures (of a leaf falling from a tree), one child replied, "Once upon a time it was fall, and there was only one leaf on the tree, and then a big wind blew it down to the ground."

When asked what other children would say if a boy came to school with only one shoe on, one child replied, "They'd say, 'ha, ha, ha.'" Then, when asked what the boy would say, he responded, "I forgot to put my other shoe on."

As these examples indicate, children by age four years and particularly by age five years are not only clear in their thinking, but are extraordinarily articulate in conveying their ideas to a listener. In general, the results suggest that at least with regard to the realm of natural discourse, the investigators who have stressed the preschoolers' verbal skills have drawn a more accurate picture than those who have emphasized their limitations. (See the controversy cited in Chapter 1.) Those who have stressed the preschoolers' weaknesses generally paint a picture of poor, almost nonexistent communication skills at age three years to beginning skills at age five years. Our results suggest, however, that the beginning skills notion is much more characteristic of the three-year-old. Further, they suggest that by age five years, the child has a sophisticated grasp of a broad and demanding range of communication skills.

In the face of such sharply divergent viewpoints, the question of what factors might be responsible for interpreting the child's behavior in such different ways inevitably arises. From our perspective, two factors seem pertinent: (1) the skill being evaluated and (2) the investigator's "adultocentrism."

The Skill Being Evaluated

The difference between the picture of limited verbal skills and the actual performance of children is typified in the reactions of people who have observed the testing. Characteristically, their comments are of the nature, "Those children are doing things that Piaget says they cannot do." In saying this, they generally have in mind the types of apparently inadequate responses that young children offer to the now classic problems of class inclusion, seriation, and conservation. Piaget's interpretations of the young child's behavior on these problems have attracted criticism from the time they were first published until now (Bryant, 1975; Isaacs, 1930; Kohnstamm, 1967). If these criticisms are valid, then they suggest that Piaget has underestimated children's ability in the realm of behavior that he is tapping.

Even should Piaget's interpretations be the more valid, however, it is important to recognize that he has focused on a particular subset of thinking—namely, the development of logical abilities. He has not dealt extensively with questions such as the ones that we have postulated are essential to natural discourse. Although his questions and ours may superficially look alike (e.g., they use phrases such as *why, how do you know,* and *will there be more*), they may be tapping different skills. The types of questions that we ask do progress along a continuum of abstraction. Nevertheless, they are still bound to the perceptual situation and do not appear to demand the level of logical thinking that Piaget's tasks are designed to measure. These comments should not be taken to mean that the possession of communication skills is trivial. In our view, such skills are an essential part of children's ability to cope with their world. Furthermore, they represent a vital element in their ability to interact with and learn from others. As such, these skills are central to the teaching situation. Issues such as communication and teaching are not and need not be of central importance to a theoretician such as Piaget who has concentrated on the development of intricate logic. However, the tone set by Piaget's interpretations may have unfortunately been extrapolated to a generalized downgrading of preschoolers' skills in areas not specifically covered by the Piagetian approach. In other words, in an effort to achieve a cohesive, parsimonious view of preschoolers, there seems to have been a neglect of the wide range of proficiencies that coexist with their limitations in functioning.

The Investigator's "Adultocentrism"

A second factor that may contribute to people's surprise at the young child's skill is the strong predilection to assess children's behavior against the yardstick of adult performance. The comparison of the child with the adult is not unreasonable since it serves as a measure of how far along a child is in a particular skill. Once the situation is formulated from this perspective, however, the conclusion almost has to be one of weakness since the child's performance rarely equals that of the adult, or even that of the older child. That the yardstick of the adult's performance is often idealized or insufficiently defined further handicaps the child. In certain cases, for instance, identical behaviors may exist in the adult and child, but because of the adultocentric bias they are interpreted differently. The child's behavior is assessed against the supposed behavior of the adult and is found wanting. By contrast, the identical behavior on the part of the adult is either unnoticed, excused, or interpreted as still further evidence for the adult's skill.

An instance of this double standard is found in the interpretation placed on children's asking of questions. It has been pointed out that our young counterparts often ask questions to which they already know the answers. (For instance, they will point to an object such as a cup and say, "What's that?" After having just asked the question, the child will then respond with the correct label if the parent replies, "Well, what is that?") Children's ability to answer the question they have asked has been interpreted to mean that they are not using questions for the mature purpose of seeking information but rather for the immature purpose of seeking attention. Hence, the child's use of questions is judged as inferior to the adult's (Chrelashviti, 1972; Lewis, 1951).

A quite different picture emerges, however, if one analyzes the questions that young children hear from adults around them. Observation of adult–child interactions shows that the adult constantly asks questions of the child to which the adult clearly knows the answer. Many traditional questions that parents initiate with children fall into this category (e.g., *what is this, where is your nose,* and *who's there*). Children's early use of questions, therefore, suggests that they are simply modeling what they have consistently seen adults do. The adults' behaviors, of course, are not interpreted as a sign of immaturity. It is *assumed* that they have a full understanding of the functions that questions serve and accordingly their behaviors are generally bypassed as not being representative of their true competence. If the adults' behaviors are analyzed at all, they may even be interpreted as a sign of sensitivity in regulating the conversation so that it will be suitable for the child.

This latter interpretation may or may not be valid. There is no reason to assume that identical behaviors need stem from the same factors or that they reflect the same basis of understanding. But equally well, it ought not to be assumed that the same behaviors reflect different underlying processes when they are carried out by a child as contrasted to their being carried out by an adult. Furthermore, there is no reason to assume that any behavior that the child executes differently from the adult is automatically inferior or inadequate. It is beyond the scope of this work to enter into a detailed analysis of these issues. Because the adult–child orientation plays such a central role in the evaluation of children, it does seem useful to offer another illustration of the problems that we have in mind.

A relevant example is available in the child's acquisition of the word "why." It has long been observed that young children (i.e., from age one and one-half years to three years) ask *why* questions in a variety of unusual circumstances—unusual, that is from the adult's perspective. For instance, an adult might say to a child, "That's the garage door." To this the child responds, "Why the garage door?" The adult's response at this point may be a somewhat puzzled, "Well it just is. That's why." Because adults would not ask such seemingly nonsensical *why's*, the child's behavior is seen as foreign and uninterpretable with the result that it either has been discarded from any analyses or has been taken as further evidence of the child's lack of mastery (Ervin-Tripp, 1970; Fahey, 1942; Lewis, 1951).

Analysis of the situation from the child's perspective leads to a different assessment. *Why* represents a difficult concept referring to an intangible referent (i.e., one cannot point to an object and say, "Here is a *why*"). When young children hear this word, they are attracted to it but lack the metalinguistics skills either to ask or interpret the answer to a question such as, "What does *why* mean?" Instead, if children are to try to understand it, they must use other techniques. This is precisely what children do. They are already knowledgeable about using question words such as *what* or *where*, which, like *why*, appear at the beginning of a question (Brown, 1968b). Hence, one of their first efforts is to attempt to use *why* in *what* and *where* type formulations (e.g., in their system they can ask, *where garage door,* so that they then try, *why garage door*). When responses to these efforts reveal that *why* cannot be used in this way (the adult seems perplexed and fails to offer an informative reply), children go on to other strategies. The intricacies of their search are too involved to discuss in detail here. (See Blank & Allen, 1976, for a detailed discussion of this process.) Suffice it to say that children use a set of coherent, reasonable, and systematic strategies that are far from being random or pointless.

The example of children's grappling with *why* points up the complexities of developmental research. On the one hand, children are by no means the equals of adults (e.g., their inability to ask directly for the meaning of the word forces them to take a long indirect route to their goal). On the other hand, they are not the bewildered organisms that the "adultocentric" view has led us to see. The influence of the "adultocentric" perspective has been so great that it is difficult to recognize the degree to which it has determined our view of the child. Its influence can perhaps best be judged by turning to a field in which a comparable approach once held sway but no longer does. The area we have in mind is that of infant research, which for many years was dominated by the notion that human infants were weak, fragile, and basically helpless organisms. They were said not to see anything but shadows at birth, not to discriminate among any sounds that they heard (except to be startled by loud noises), and so on. This view has shifted dramatically within the past two decades. Partly because of more inventive assessment procedures (Eimas, 1975; Fantz, 1961; and Haith et al., 1969) and partly because of Piaget's (1952) emphasis on the infant as an active problem-solver, the human infant has now come to be thought of as far more capable and skilled than was ever imagined. Indeed, a major book in the area is *The Competent Infant* (Stone et al., 1973). (Also see Kuhn, 1962, for a discussion of the changes in the conceptual framework in scientific research.)

Somewhat surprisingly, a comparable shift—from a view of incompetence to one of competence—has not taken place for preschool-age children even though they are far more skilled than infants. There are beginning signs that such a shift may be underway (e.g., the references in Chapter 1 on the preschoolers' verbal skills represent elements of this shift). In emphasizing this point, we do not mean that preschoolers should be seen only from the viewpoint of strength. Rather, we are saying that an adequate representation of young children requires that we overcome the dominance of the "adultocentric" perspective and incorporate other approaches that will reveal the skills that they clearly possess but which have long been overlooked.

Criterion-referenced testing holds promise in this regard, since it permits the child to be assessed not against the adult, or older child, but rather against a criterion of effective performance on any set of skills. Its potential for expanding our view of the child has led us to adopt the concept of mastery in assessing the children's skills. Future work may show the need for revising the criterion that we have selected (e.g., children who achieve the 50 percent or even the 67 percent criterion in all four groups of discourse skills may not be found to be sufficiently proficient in coping with naturally occurring dialogue, and different criteria may have to be chosen). However, the concept of mastery does provide the basis for a wider and more accurate assessment of the preschooler's range of abilities and limitations.

A COMPARISON OF THE TWO SOCIAL CLASSES

Until this point the discussion has emphasized the relatively high percentage of children who attain mastery in discourse by the end of the preschool years. As indicated in Figure 5-1, however, not all children dem-

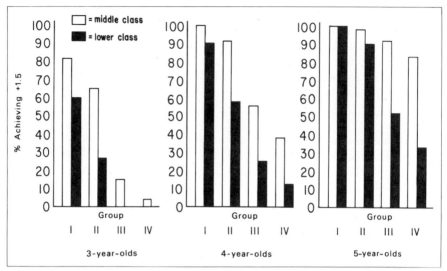

Figure 5-3   *Percentage of middle- and lower-class children achieving above 1.5 criterion at each age.*

onstrate proficiency in communication. For example, approximately 42 percent of the five-year-olds achieved scores below the 1.5 criterion on the Group IV demands. For many of that group (i.e., about a third of the 42 percent) the scores are even below 1.0. (A score lower than 1.0 reflects the presence of adequate responses to fewer than a third of the Group IV demands.)

Given the issues that have motivated this research, the question that arises at this point is whether or not the differences in performance are related to the children's social class background. As a first step in answering this question, we have again examined the percentages of children who attain the 50 percent criterion of mastery. This time, however, the data are separated according to whether the children are from the middle or lower classes. The results derived from this analysis are shown in Figure 5-3, in which wide and consistent differences can be seen between the two groups of children at all ages on all four groups of tasks. One of the most revealing comparisons is the extent of the difference between the two groups of five-year-olds (they represent the group that is about to enter first grade). Using the criterion of 50 percent mastery, we find that 40 of the 48, or 83 percent of the middle-class five-year-olds have attained this level of performance on all four groups of discourse skills (i.e., each of the 40 attained scores of 1.5 or greater on all four groups of items). By contrast, among the lower-class five-year-olds, the figures are 16 out of 48, or 33 percent.[2] If we set as our criterion of mastery the 67 percent level (i.e., a

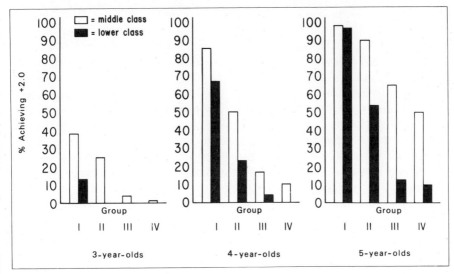

Figure 5-4   *Percentage of middle- and lower-class children achieving above 2.0 criterion* at each age.

score of 2.0), we find that 24 of the middle-class children attain this level on all four groups while only 5 of the lower-class children do. These figures represent 50 percent and 10 percent of the groups respectively and are shown in Figure 5-4.

The differences between the classes can also be seen in the children's performance on the individual items within each group of discourse skills. A detailed presentation of the children's performance on the individual processes is available in Appendix C.[3] Here, we wish simply to highlight

---

[2]These percentages differ slightly from the percentages in Figure 5-3. The percentages in the text are based on the numbers of children who achieved scores above 1.5 on *all* four groups. By contrast, the percentages shown in the figures reflect the performance on *each* of the four groups separately. For example, a particular child might have a Group III score of 1.8 and a Group IV score of 1.2. The 1.8 score would enter into the percentages on Figure 5-3 since it is above the 1.5 criterion. That score, however, would not enter into the percentages cited in the text since all of that child's scores were not above 1.5.

[3]Because such a varied number of processes have been tested in each group, it is possible to carry out extensive analyses of the children's performance on individual tasks. For example, the concept of exclusion has been studied through a number of Group III tasks. As a result, it is possible to evaluate how the children's response to this concept is affected by the particular task in which it is embedded, for example, dces the presence or absence of materials affect the child's ability to deal with exclusion? Because the amount of material to be covered here is extensive, it is not possible to analyze the various tasks in a detailed manner in this book. However, it is planned to present further analyses of the results in reports and papers to be published in appropriate journals.

some of the findings. For example, on the 43 items of Group IV, Adequate responses were offered to *every item* by over half of the middle-class five-year-olds. By contrast, among the lower-class five-year-olds, 19 of the 43 items received fewer than 50 percent Adequate responses. These results suggest that the great majority of middle-class children in our sample seem ready to deal with the full range of discourse that they experience in the school setting, while only a minority of the lower-class children display this level of performance. The minority, however, is a sizeable one, that is, 33 percent of the lower-class children in our sample do achieve the 1.5 criterion and the presence of this group should not be downplayed. An unfortunate byproduct of any analyses of performance among lower-class children is the tendency to overlook the high level of functioning that is attained by many children from that background, with the result that little effort is expended in capitalizing on their skills.

Differences are also found in the performance of the two social classes on the Group I and II demands. In terms of the 50 percent criterion, however, the differences do not seem to be of major importance (e.g., at five years the 1.5 criterion on Groups I and II is attained by 100 percent and 98 percent, respectively, of the middle-class children; for the lower class, the figures are 100 percent and 90 percent, respectively). The striking differences, for the five-year-olds at least, appear to be found in the Group III and IV demands. As described earlier, the Group III and IV demands require the children to restructure and reason about their experiences. For the most part, these demands are realized in tasks that contain formulations such as *if—then, why, think about what happens,* and *how do you know.* These sorts of questions have often been deemed vital to the development of critical thinking, and teachers are exhorted to ask as many of these questions as possible (Flanders, 1970; Taba & Elkins, 1966). Our results indicate, however, that a high percentage of children from lower-class backgrounds cannot grapple with these questions when they are ready to enter first grade. Accordingly, the posing of such problems does not appear to stimulate thought; rather, it serves only to stimulate confusion and error. These findings may well explain the seemingly paradoxical result (Soar & Soar, 1976) that in classes in which teachers ask higher level questions, the students' achievement levels are often lower. It appears that confrontation with the full and supposedly more stimulating range of discourse demands leads the children to increased failure.

In evaluating the discourse skills of children, our discussion has been based on the numbers of children who perform above and below criterion. The use of this cutoff point provides no indication of the magnitude of the differences in the scores between the groups (i.e., they do not indicate if the differences in the absolute scores are wide or narrow). In order to

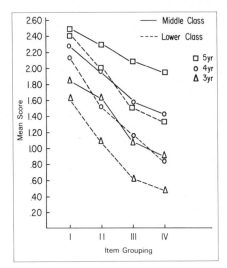

Figure 5-5 *Test performance of children by age and socioeconomic status.*

examine this aspect of the results, the children's mean scores on each of the four groups of tasks have been calculated. The means, which have been computed separately according to the children's age and socioeconomic background, are plotted in Figure 5-5. They indicate that wide differences exist on all four groups of tasks at all ages. In general, the differences in performance between the two social classes average about one year. That is, four-year-old lower-class children respond in ways similar to three-year-old middle-class children, while the five-year-old lower-class children respond in ways similar to the four-year-old middle-class children.[4]

Although differences between the children's scores occur for all four groups of tasks, the differences are not uniform in each of the four groups. The differences between the Group I scores for the two social classes are

---

[4]As tested by analysis of variance, the difference between the performance of the two classes is significant at $p < .001$. Interestingly, analysis of the data also indicates that there is a significant difference in performance according to sex, with girls obtaining higher scores than boys. As noted in Chapter 4, however, girls also have slightly higher IQ scores than do boys. To equate for this, analysis of covariance has been carried out, with IQ being the covariate. When this is done, differences in test performance according to sex are no longer found to be significant. These results are similar to those reported in other studies, particularly those on lower-class children. In those studies, it has been found that lower-class preschool-age girls tend to perform more successfully on language-based tasks than do their male counterparts. (See Maccoby & Jacklin, 1974 for an extended review of this topic.) The analysis of variance is shown in detail in Appendix D.

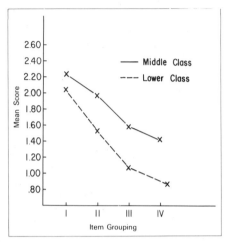

Figure 5-6   *Test performance of children by socioeconomic status.*

quite small. For example, across the three ages, the average difference for Group I scores between middle- and lower-class children is 0.16. However, the differences become wider as the demands increase in the level of abstraction. Thus, the average difference for Group II scores between the two classes at all ages is 0.46, for Group III scores it is 0.49, and for Group IV scores it is 0.55. These results are depicted in Figure 5-6 in which the overall pattern of performance on the four groups of tasks is graphed for the middle- and lower-class children for all ages combined. The figure shows that the difference between the middle and lower class is relatively small on Group I items and then progressively increases for the other groups of items, so that at Group IV the difference between the classes is at its greatest.

At first glance, one might suspect that the results shown are due to a "ceiling effect"; that is, the Group I items are so easy that everyone achieves the highest score possible and so minimal differences are found. This explanation, however, does not seem adequate. Group I performance continues to improve from age three to four to five years. In other words, even when the children have not yet attained their highest performance, differences between the classes on Group I performance are less marked than are differences on Group IV performance. Statistical analysis indicates that this difference in patterning is significant.[5]

---

[5]As assessed by a three-way repeated measures analysis of variance, the differences in class, age, and Group I to IV scores are significant at $p < .001$, the interaction between class and Group I to IV scores and the interaction between age and Group I to IV scores are both significant at $p < .001$, and finally, the interaction between class, age, and Group I to IV scores is significant at $p < .002$. (See Appendix D for the full presentation of the analysis.)

These results parallel the findings of Joan Tough (1977), who reports different predispositions in the use of language among three-year-old British children from middle- and working-class backgrounds. The working-class children use speech to a much greater extent for what is termed the "self-maintaining use of language." This use reflects the expression of needs (e.g., *I want a sweet*) and the protection of interests (e.g., *go away—you're hurting me*). Language of this sort is comparable in level of abstraction to Group I demands since it entails a high correspondence between the words and the ideas being reported. By contrast, middle-class children are found to be more disposed to use language for "extending and promoting action" and for "securing collaboration with others." Encompassed within these functions are predictions (e.g., *my daddy will be coming soon, and then I'm going home with him*), imaginative play episodes (e.g., *that's a hospital now*), and statements of reasoning (e.g., *somebody must have dropped it*). These uses of language appear to correspond to Group III and IV type demands in which there is an increasing distance between the language and the material that are immediately evident to the child.

Given the prominence that is currently accorded to the theme of cultural difference, it is tempting to speculate as to how these differences may reflect differences in communication styles of various cultural groups. Before following that course, however, it is necessary to determine whether factors other than social class could account for the findings. The major factor that comes to mind is the children's IQ level. As pointed out in Chapter 4, a significant difference of about 15 IQ points exists between the two groups of children in our sample. Given the importance of IQ on task performance, it could well be that the differences in patterning are simply a reflection of differences in IQ. That is, the higher the IQ, the relatively higher the performance on Group IV; the lower the IQ, the relatively higher the performance on Group I. Since middle-class children have higher IQs, they could be expected to score disproportionately well on Group IV items, and similarly, the lower-class children with their lower IQs could be expected to perform disproportionately well on Group I items.

In order to see if the differences between the social classes would be maintained even if there were no IQ differences, a group of 45 pairs of children from the total sample has been compared. One member of each pair comes from a lower-class background and the other member comes from a middle-class background. Each pair is matched in IQ. The difference in IQ across the 45 pairs averages 2.6 points and never exceeds 7.0 points for any pair of children. In addition, the two children in each pair are nearly the same age (they were born within one month of each other) and are of the same sex. A plot of their group scores is shown in Figure 5-7, in which it can be seen that only a narrow gap exists between the perfor-

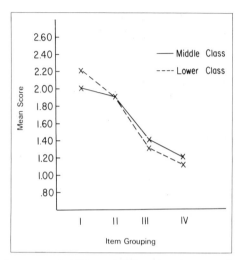

Figure 5-7   *Test performance of children of different socioeconomic status matched for IQ.*

mance of the lower- and middle-class children. Thus, when the children are matched for IQ, the wide differences in performance between the social classes are no longer found. These results suggest that, to a considerable degree, the difference in performance between the two social classes is related to differences in IQ.

Of interest to our discussion here, however, is that the full extent of the differences cannot be accounted for in this way. The differences in the pattern of Group I to IV scores that are seen when the total sample is studied remain when the comparison involves children who are matched for IQ.[6] Indeed, the lower-class children not only do relatively well on Group I, but they achieve higher scores than do the middle class on this group of items. On Groups III and IV, however, the previously noted differences between the classes is maintained, with the lower-class child still doing less well than the middle-class child. These differences are statistically significant.[7] These results suggest that if no differences in IQ existed

---

[6]As assessed by a three-way repeated measures analysis of variance, there are no significant differences according to class ($p > .05$) when the children are matched for IQ. There is, however, a significant interaction between class and Group scores ($p < .01$), reflecting the different pattern of performance displayed by the two classes. (See Appendix D for the presentation of the analysis.)

[7]The role of IQ has also been assessed through an analysis of covariance on the total sample of 288 children, with IQ serving as the covariate. On this analysis, the same results are found as with the matched pairs analysis of variance: There are no overall class differences, but there is a Class by Group score interaction ($p < .001$). The interaction reflects the different pattern shown by the children of the two social classes on the Group I to IV scores, with the lower-class children doing relatively better on Group I items and the middle class doing better on Group III and IV items. (See Appendix D.)

between the classes, the lower-class child would be slightly superior to the middle-class child in Group I type skills but would continue to be slightly less proficient in Group III and IV skills. These results further suggest that children of different social class backgrounds are disposed to approach discourse demands in somewhat different ways. Lower-class children become increasingly proficient in attending to and describing the world just before them; middle-class children become increasingly proficient in using language as a tool to restructure and reason about their perception.

Although these differences are intriguing, it is important to note that their effect in any situation would be relatively small. For example, let us imagine that there are two five-year-old children with IQs of 125, one from a lower-class background and the other from a middle-class background. While each might show the differential performance in the Group I and IV areas, the major feature of their performance would be its similarity, not its difference. Both would be likely to display high levels of mastery across the range of discourse skills, and the differences in their performance would probably not hamper their generally good ability to understand and benefit from the classroom exchange.

THE QUALITY OF THE RESPONSE

Given the significant correlation between performances on the intelligence test and on the discourse test, the question that arises is what is achieved by using the discourse test rather than an IQ test. The answer rests on the use to which the information can be put. While IQ tests correlate with school performance, their design does not permit one to identify the specific factors that are responsible for the difficulties of children who perform poorly in the school setting or for the success of those who perform well. As a result, they fail to indicate how the teacher might modify the interaction with the child so as to facilitate learning. By contrast, the discourse test is specifically directed toward this problem. The level and patterning of performance that a child displays on the four groups of discourse skills help to pinpoint the difficulties that a child may encounter in interaction with the teacher.

The discourse test has also been designed to provide additional information that will be of use in the practical setting. As described in Chapter 3, children may display a number of different reactions to any demand. For example, when asked a question such as, *what will happen when I put this (a small object) on this side of the scale,* they may sit and say nothing, venture a guess and suggest that the scale will not move, or speak in a way that is unrelated to the problem (e.g., *I got toys at home*). In the emphasis on achieving "right answers" in the school setting, there has often been serious neglect of these various levels of "wrong answers." Wrong answers, however, are critical in offering us insights into the children's understanding of a problem and in determining what a teacher can or should do in the ensuing dialogue: For example, if the interaction is to be meaningful, a teacher's response to a reply such as, *I got toys at home,* should be quite different from the response to an answer such as, *it won't move* (Blank, 1973). As such, the quality of the child's response plays a vital role in any effort directed towards understanding the teaching process. As outlined in Chapter 3, information on this aspect of the child's behavior is available in the 10-point Quality of the Response scale. (See Table 3-1.)

In organizing the information yielded by this scale, it is useful to study the way in which the children's responses distribute themselves over the various categories. This information cannot be derived by simply examining the absolute number of responses in each category. Since lower-class children offer many more Inadequate responses than middle-class children do, any use of absolute number would only show lower-class children having more Inadequate responses in every category. In order to gain a more informative picture of the pattern of responses, we have calculated the percentage of each type of Inadequate response made by every child (i.e., the percentage of a child's Inadequate responses that are Invalid, Associated, and so on). For purposes of illustration, let us examine the range of responses that a child has offered to the 34 items of Group I. Suppose that in response to these items, a child has offered 16 Inadequate responses, which are distributed as follows: 2 Invalid, 8 Associated, 0 Irrelevant, and 6 I Don't Know. The child's percentages in the various categories of Inadequate responses would, accordingly, be 13 percent Invalid, 50 percent Associated, 0 percent Irrelevant, and 38 percent I Don't Know. This type of computation has been carried out for each child in the study, and in all cases it has been computed separately for each of the four groups of items. The groups have been treated separately since each represents a different set of skills.

The results of this analysis are shown in Figures 5-8 through 5-12.[8] The highest level of Inadequate responses are represented by the Invalid and Associated categories. While Associated responses were much more frequent than Invalid responses, both tended to increase with age for both social classes. For example, when the Invalid and Associated responses are combined (i.e., the percentage of Invalid and Associated responses for Group I items, for Group II items, and so forth), we find that at age three years, the children (both lower- and middle-class) have 30 percent to 42

---

[8]For certain categories, there are no entries on the graph because no responses of that type were offered by the particular subgroup of children. For example, neither the five-year-old lower-class or middle-class children made any Invalid or Associated responses to the Group I items. Rather than attempt to indicate 0 percent, the figure was left empty at that point.

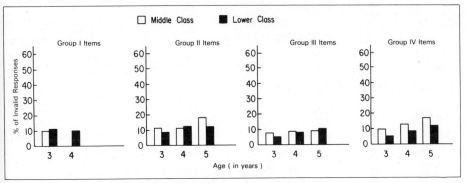

Figure 5-8   *Distribution of Invalid responses by age and socioeconomic status.*

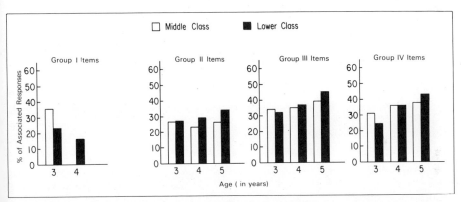

Figure 5-9   *Distribution of Associated responses by age and socioeconomic status.*

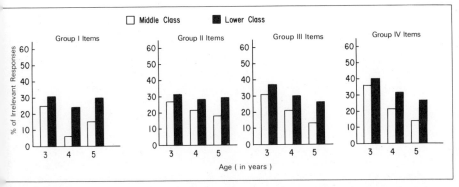

Figure 5-10   *Distribution of Irrelevant responses by age and socioeconomic status.*

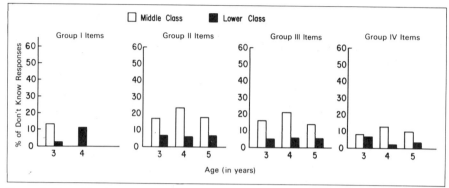

Figure 5-11   *Distribution of I Don't Know responses by age and socioeconomic status.*

percent of their Inadequate responses in these categories: at age four years, 34 percent to 49 percent, and at age five years, 44 percent to 55 percent. This result indicates that as the children grow older, fewer of their Inadequate responses are in the lower level categories and more are in the higher level categories. In other words, even when they are incorrect, the older children offer responses that are closer to the information demanded by the question. While there is a trend for the middle-class children to offer relatively more Invalid responses and for the lower-class children to offer relatively more Associated responses, the general pattern of responses on these categories for the two social classes is similar.

The picture for the Irrelevant response, however, is different. The Irrelevant response is one in which the children offer no sign that they have understood either the problem posed or the material that is contained within the problem. Frequently, the answers involve comments about important people in their lives *(my daddy got that)*, imitations of part of what the tester has said *(find it)*, or denials of the problem *(there is no picture)*.

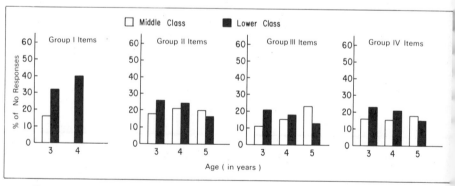

Figure 5-12   *Distribution of No Response by age and socioeconomic status.*

For both social classes, Irrelevant responses generally decrease with age. But at all ages, and on all groups of items, lower-class children offer more Irrelevant responses than do middle-class children. Further, the difference increases with age; that is, the decline in these responses among the middle class is more marked than among the lower class. Thus, at age three years, the average difference between the middle-class and lower-class percentages of Irrelevant responses is 5 percent (averaged across the four groups of tasks), at age four years it is 9 percent, and at age five years, it is 13 percent (see Figure 5-10). These figures represent the percentage of Inadequate responses that fall into the Irrelevant category. In terms of absolute numbers, the discrepancy between the social classes would be much higher since lower-class children give more Inadequate responses overall. Accordingly, their total number of Irrelevant responses would be greater.

Anyone who has observed conversations between adults and children will recognize the disruptive effects that irrelevant comments have on the flow of the dialogue. For example, in one class, a teacher was observed to ask a child, "What did you see at the zoo yesterday?" He responded, "I ate 12 hot dogs." The teacher looked bewildered and immediately countered with, "Oh no, you couldn't have." The teacher almost certainly had not intended to offer this reply, for this was a teacher who prided herself on never rejecting anything that a child said to her. Although her response betrayed her philosophy, it was not at all atypical or unexpected. Rather, it reflected the confusion that adults experience when confronted with responses of this sort. Invariably, the adult is disconcerted by the child's comment and does not know what to say to help the child understand the discussion at hand. The end result is that the exchange often ends in an abrupt and frustrating manner as the adult registers surprise (e.g., a rather fumbling and disbelieving agreement such as, *did you really?*) or rejection (e.g., a seemingly gentle, but clear statement of denial such as, *oh, I'm sure you didn't eat that many*).

While Irrelevant responses are signs of confusion on the children's part, at the same time they are signs of their active participation in the dialogue. As such, the presence of many of these responses among lower-class children stands in sharp contrast to the picture that has frequently been painted of their behavior in testing or classroom situations. In these reports, it has been suggested that these children perform poorly because they are threatened by questions and therefore say nothing (Cazden et al., 1972; Labov, 1969). The following quote is illustrative of this viewpoint.

The results . . . suggest that the child knows the relevant information but does not communicate it. This may occur because he views the classroom situation as threatening and says nothing . . . or because he as-

sumes that the teacher already knows the answer and it would be redundant for him to tell her what she already knows. (Bruck & Tucker, 1974, p. 217)

Our results do not support these contentions. Indeed, if we contrast the Irrelevant category with the I Don't Know and No Response categories (the categories that are indicative of the child not offering specific responses), the picture we see is almost diametrically opposed to the speculations in the literature. For example, when the I Don't Know and No Response categories are combined, we find that on all groups of items and at all ages, the middle-class children have higher percentages of these responses than lower-class children do. Further, the differences increase with age. Thus, at age three years, the average difference between the classes (across all groups of items) on the I Don't Know and No Responses is 3 percent, at age four years, it is 9 percent, and at age five years, it is 14 percent. In all cases, it is the middle-class child who offers the greatest numbers of refusals to respond. From these results, it appears that when a difficult problem is posed that is beyond the child's comprehension, the lower-class child is more likely to offer Irrelevant Responses, and the middle-class child is more likely to refuse to venture an answer. The reasons for this difference remain to be determined. It may be that middle-class children are far more concerned about being right. As a result, when confronted with a situation in which they are unsure of the correct response middle-class children are more inhibited about revealing their thoughts on the problem. Alternatively, this behavior may be seen as a sign that middle-class children are less concerned about admitting their ignorance. (These opposing but nonetheless reasonable alternatives illustrate the difficulties in evaluating young children's behaviors.) Regardless of the interpretation, our findings suggest that lower-class preschool-age children as a group are not inhibited and withdrawn in the testing situation. If anything, they are freer in expressing their thoughts and ideas than the middle-class children are. At a minimum, these findings question the reported phenomenon of withdrawal and inhibition in the presence of a white, middle-class adult (examiner or teacher) and suggest that it deserves far more extensive study with large numbers of children drawn from a variety of ages.

Where our results and the speculations in the literature agree is in the relative balance of I Don't Know and No Response. When middle-class children fail to offer a specific answer, they are more likely to say, "I don't know"; in the same situation, lower-class children are more likely to say nothing or simply to shrug. From the listener's perspective, silence in response to a question is more disturbing than is a response such as, *I don't know,* or *I don't remember.* If others are present (as they usually are in the teaching situation), the discomfort is invariably relieved by the questioner, that is, the teacher turning to someone else in order to continue the exchange. On the other hand, a response of *I don't know* seems to be interpreted more readily as an indication that the child has been listening and is interested in maintaining contact with the questioner. This interpretation may or may not be valid. In the school setting, for example, verbal answers may be overvalued, even when the answers are *I don't know*. But should this predisposition exist, it could be a factor leading to bias in the teacher's estimate of the child's ability.

An interesting sidelight to the analysis is that the pattern of Inadequate responses that is found in the two social classes is maintained when the comparison is restricted to the 45 pairs of children matched for IQ. As noted earlier, one member of each pair is middle-class and the other is lower-class. There are 15 pairs each at ages three, four, and five years. The distribution of their responses is shown in Figure 5-13, in which the following characteristics can be seen. First, the children from both classes show a decline in Irrelevant responses as they progress from age three to five years. However, the decline is again more marked in the middle-class children, so that at age five years, the lower-class children show a mean of 23 percent Irrelevant responses while the middle-class children show a mean of 14 percent. Second, the middle-class children also show a higher level of I Don't Know responses than do the lower-class children. For example, at age five years, the respective figures are 17 percent and 9 percent. The groups do not differ sharply in the percentages of No Response. These results suggest that the different patterning of Inadequate responses is dependent not on IQ but on social class factors. As indicated in the examples here, the presence of these differences may well affect both the flow of the dialogue and the teacher's evaluation of the child's behavior. The precise role that they play, however, can only be determined by further study.

KNOWING ABOUT VERSUS TALKING ABOUT

Although the analysis of Inadequate responses is revealing, it does not answer a difficult question that is often raised when evaluating children's failures, namely why the child is not giving an appropriate or adequate response. In considering this question, it is important to keep in mind that an Adequate response requires two basic sets of skills. It requires first an understanding of the situation confronting the child, and second, the ability to talk about or communicate this understanding. When poor performance is attained in a group of discourse skills, it is not possible to

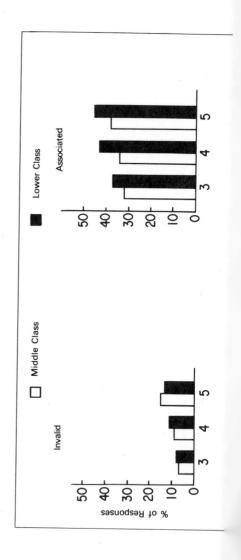

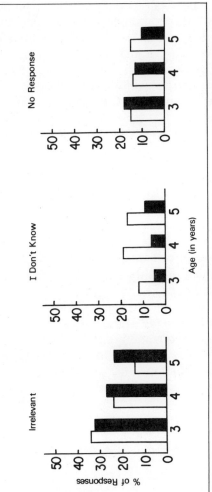

Figure 5-13 *Distribution of types of Inadequate responses across all groups of Items in children matched for IQ from different socioeconomic backrounds.*

know whether the difficulties stem from either or both of these factors. Interestingly, one's approach to this problem seems to depend on the theoretical perspective, or bias, that one holds. For example, teachers commonly take the position that any difficulties stem predominantly from the second component; that is, the ability to talk about one's knowledge. Thus, if a child is asked to describe what is happening in a picture and responds by simply labeling an object (e.g., *a lady*), a teacher will typically comment, "Oh, I'm sure he knows the answer, he just can't tell you exactly what he means."

The problems with this interpretation rest not with its validity but rather with its implied judgment that "talking about" is inconsequential. In the teacher's view, it is sufficient as long as he or she feels that the child knows the information. Overlooked is that just being unable to talk about the subject represents a major weakness. That is, the children are in a position in which they are not accessible to dialogue with others, with the result that a major channel for learning is severed.

In contrast to this approach, other specialists often assume that the talking about component is functioning well and that any failure is due to the child's weakness in the knowledge base. This predisposition is evidenced in Piaget's work on conservation in which, children are judged *not* to possess the concept unless they can justify the responses that they have given. For example, if children say that two rows of six buttons continue to be equal (after one row has been spread out to be longer than the other), they may still be judged to be at a preconservation stage if they cannot answer the question, *why are they still the same?* The use of *same* in this context is a level III demand, while the *why* question represents a level IV demand. When young children fail this question, therefore, it may not be that they are unable to conserve but rather that they are unable to talk about their understanding since it requires a facility in level III and IV demands. that they may not yet possess. Thus, what seems to be a fairly straightforward task in which the communication aspect can be assumed to pose no problems is in fact a highly intricate task requiring much further analysis. (See Goodnow, 1973, and Rose & Blank, 1974, for experimental work illustrating the ideas just discussed.)

While it is important to know whether the children's difficulties in any area are caused by their lack of understanding or their inability to talk about their understanding, it is unlikely that a solution will soon be forthcoming. One obstacle is that in many situations, verbal behavior cannot be adequately assessed without consideration of the accompanying nonverbal behavior. Thus far, the potentially revealing nonverbal behavior has scarcely been examined. This point can be illustrated through an example of interactions that have occurred in our teaching of the children (Blank,

1973). For instance, in one situation a child may be asked to find a cup to hold some juice. Two paper cups are available, one with a bottom and one without. Several types of responses are possible and we will confine our comments here to just two. Some children, when confronted with this problem, choose the cup with the bottom missing. They seem totally comfortable with this selection, and even if they are asked whether or not they are sure that they can use this cup, they answer *yes* and evidence no signs of doubt. When the juice is poured into the cup, they still show no surprise and simply say something such as, *the juice won't stay in.* This behavior seems to reflect a weakness in the prerequisite understanding of the material that must exist before any meaningful "talking about" of the problem can take place.

In contrast, other children select the cup with the bottom. When asked why they chose that cup (a Group IV demand), they seem to want to formulate a response but are unable to do so. It might then be suggested that they try the other cup. The children go along with the suggestion, that is, they use the cup without the bottom, because they are uncomfortable in challenging an adult authority figure. However, it is clear from their discomfort that at some level they know that the choice will not function effectively, but they cannot verbalize *why.* Behavioral responses such as these (e.g., the presence or absence of discomfort with the inappropriate) might thus be able to serve as guides in evaluating whether the source of children's difficulties is in the realm of understanding or talking about that understanding or both. There has been relatively little work in the integration of verbal and nonverbal behaviors in assessing a child's level of awareness. (See Charlesworth, 1969, Gelman, 1972, and Shantz & Watson, 1970, for further discussion of this topic.) We present this issue here not because we can offer any guidelines as to how to proceed, but rather to illustrate the importance of beginning to deal with this problem. Should an integration of the verbal and nonverbal behaviors be achieved, it will almost certainly lead to a much clearer picture of the skills that young children possess.

SUMMARY

This chapter has been directed toward answering two questions that are basic to the research we have been conducting: (1) whether or not preschool children have mastery over the range of discourse skills that are necessary for teacher–child communication and (2) to what extent differences in the mastery of such skills are associated with social class background.

In summarizing the results, it seems useful to return to these questions and use them as a framework for presenting the major findings. Our results indicate that many preschoolers do have an excellent grasp of the range of discourse skills. Using a criterion of 50 percent as indicating a working mastery of an area, we find that by age three years, 71 percent and 46 percent, respectively, of the children have achieved that criterion on Group I and II skills. By age five years, mastery on the Group III and IV skills is evidenced by 72 percent and 58 percent respectively. With mastery of the four groups, the children are essentially able to deal with the entire range of discourse demands that occur in school-based dialogue.

The mastery of the range of discourse skills, however, is not uniformly achieved in children of the two social classes. In general, by age five years, the great majority of middle-class children have achieved mastery over the four groups of discourse skills, while among lower-class children only a minority have achieved similar levels of mastery. For example, among the five-year-olds, 83 percent of the middle-class children have achieved the 50 percent criterion on all four groups, as compared to 33 percent of the lower-class children. Many of the differences between the achievement of lower-class and middle-class children are related to IQ differences. That is, when the children are matched for IQ, the wide gap in performance between the two social classes is not as evident. Nevertheless, even when the children are equated for IQ, some differences in performance still exist. In particular, lower-class children perform relatively better on Group I skills than do middle-class children, while the reverse is true for Group IV skills.

Analysis of the quality of the response also yields interesting differences between the social classes. For both groups of children, the greatest percentage of their Inadequate responses are in the Invalid and Associated categories. This indicates that even when children experience difficulty in offering Adequate answers, almost all of them are focused on the task and attempt to deal with it as best they can. However, beyond these categories there are differences between the classes. The lower-class child tends to give more Irrelevant responses than does the middle-class child who, in turn, tends to give many more answers that fall in the I Don't Know and No Response categories. These results run counter to speculations that have pictured the lower-class child as withdrawing into silence when confronted with school-type demands.

6

What Can Be Done?

THE QUESTION OF FEASIBILITY

In this chapter we will examine the implications that the test results hold for the education of young children. The first question that will be considered is the basic one of feasibility. As stated in Chapter 1, contradictory reports of preschoolers' language skills have raised doubts about the extent of their ability to benefit from the classroom exchange. Although the test results show important differences in performance according to age and social class background, we nevertheless believe that they can be taken to support the view that preschool-age children possess sufficient skill in discourse to allow formal educational efforts to be productive. Indeed, the verbal skills of many four- and five-year-old children are so extensive and sophisticated that there seems to be little doubt of their ability to engage in meaningful, varied, and sustained interchanges with teachers. For these children formal educational programs would seem to be entirely feasible.

For other children, the issue of preschool education is somewhat less straightforward. All the children in our sample have shown themselves to be able to cope effectively with aspects of the continuum of discourse. In that sense, all of them would seem to be able to deal with elements of the formal educational exchange, regardless of age and socioeconomic background. But this conclusion does not mean that there is agreement on whether preschool education should be implemented for these children, and if so, what the goals of such programs should be. In education, the conclusions that one reaches are frequently based not simply on data but also (and perhaps to a far greater extent) on the philosophy that one holds concerning what schools can or should do. A case in point is the long-dominant educational model that Glaser (1976) has termed the *Selec-*

tive Fixed Track. In this model, which was developed when education was geared to the training of a small elite, children are selected for school only if they show a high level of performance on the skills that are deemed vital for academic success. The school system makes little or no attempt either to help children who do not have the skills or to modify its demands to capitalize on the alternative skills that such children may possess. Were this model to be adopted here, it would mean that those children who are weak in discourse skills would be screened out as unable to profit from the preschool situation. With this philosophy the question of feasibility is then resolved in the negative. Formal education is deemed inappropriate and not useful for the children in question.

This sort of conclusion does not have to mean that quality education be permanently denied to these children. One might simply wait until they developed the prerequisite skills before enrolling them in a formal program. Given the history of efforts spawned under the Selective Fixed Track model, however, permanent denial of opportunity is a likely outcome. This potential abuse stems from the fact that within this framework, the school feels free to concentrate its efforts on the children who are likely to do well. As a result, any labeling of the children at entry to indicate weakness serves not for positive diagnostic purposes but rather as a rationalization for denying them productive opportunities throughout their school lives.[1]

Because of abuses that it has fostered, there has been a growing dissatisfaction with the Selective Fixed Track model. Many educators have abandoned it in favor of what are seen as more productive alternatives. One such alternative has been termed the *Development of Initial Competence.* In this approach, the school attempts to help children modify their "cognitive processes so that [they] can meet the demands of the learning environment" (Glaser, 1976, p. 350). That is, the curriculum is geared to helping children develop the skills in which they are weak. In a second alternative, termed *Accommodation to Different Styles of Learning,* the school identifies the talents that children possess and then designs the curriculum to capitalize on these talents; that is, the curriculum is geared to the child's previously developed strengths.

Despite their differences, both models share the idea that the curriculum can be modified to offer appropriate educational opportunities to all chil-

---

[1]Implementation of this model requires that there be some means for identifying those children who will and those who will not succeed in school. Much of the early testing effort, such as that of Binet and Simon (1916), owes its development to this philosophy. Once classified, the child can be, and often is, simply kept out of the mainstream of the school (Anastasi, 1961, and Mercer, 1973). This use of testing has led many to disparage the giving of any tests in school.

dren. The school experiences that will result in each case, however, will be distinctly different. This can be seen by applying each approach to the issues of preschool education that we have been considering. On the one hand, if the model selected is designed to develop initial competence, a central task becomes one of enhancing and expanding the child's range of discourse skills. On the other hand, if the model selected is designed to accommodate different styles of learning, a central task becomes one of molding the language exchange so that all dialogue is consonant with the child's already existing skills. The attainment of either objective is difficult and involves, at a minimum, expertise in complex issues such as task analysis, teacher retraining, and the introduction of alternative curriculum content. These issues are beyond the scope of this work. It is feasible, however, to sketch some of the ways in which the model of discourse and the test results may be used in meeting these objectives.

DEVELOPMENT OF INITIAL COMPETENCE

Let us consider first the implications of a strategy for developing initial competence. In the domain of discourse, this approach leads to a concentration on techniques that enhance the child's skills in communication. In other words, the generally unnoticed medium of classroom exchange is transformed to become the content of the teaching. Difficulties arise, however, in knowing how to enhance the child's skill in this area. It is well recognized in education that there is a vast difference between knowing what one wishes students to learn and knowing the strategies for allowing them to learn it (Glaser, 1973; Scandura, 1977). Many educators, for example, value curiosity in the child and accordingly make it a goal of many programs. Yet there are no known definite techniques or methods by which this goal may be attained. In place of knowledge, we frequently find a chasm between the objectives and the means to these objectives.

In the area of discourse, the difficulties are compounded because the generally accepted means for teaching discourse paradoxically demand precisely the skills that the children do not have. For instance, it is commonly maintained that children's language skills will be increased if they are presented with stimulating questions, particularly questions that demand problem solving (Barnes, 1969; Flanders, 1970; Moffett, 1968; Robison, 1977; Taba, 1966). For reasons that are far from proven, it seems to have been assumed that the asking of a "good" (i.e., higher level) question will produce "those mental activities demanded by the inquiry" (Sigel & Cocking, 1977, p. 213). Our results indicate, however, that asking such questions of children who are weak in discourse serves not to stimulate thought but rather to provoke failure (i.e., it leads to many inadequate responses). The conclusion that one must draw from this analysis is that the commonly prescribed path for facilitating discourse skills seems inappropriate for the young children most in need of this facilitation.

The problem of teacher-induced failure is not unique to the realm of discourse. In education, and particularly in special education, instruction is based on the formula of "assume the paths the learner already knows and concentrate on those that he or she does not [know]" (Scandura, 1977, p. 41). A concentration on what the child does not know is almost bound to lead to failure. Recognition of this problem is in large measure responsible for the popularity of task analysis (Gagné, 1970). The idea is that failure accompanying the learning of a new skill can be minimized if one identifies the hierarchy of component parts contained within any skill. Once these parts are identified, each can be systematically introduced to the child only after he or she has mastered the preceding components in the hierarchy. Hence, the amount of teacher-induced failure is kept to a minimum.

While a task-analysis approach has been useful in a number of areas, little of it has been directed at dissecting the subcomponents of conversational exchanges, such as those that a teacher uses with children. As occurred in our test of discourse, for example, preschoolers may systematically fail *why* questions because they do not understand the factors entailed in formulating an acceptable answer to this question. (See Blank & Allen, 1976, for a fuller discussion of this issue.) Task analysis offers almost no guidelines on how an intangible concept such as *why* can be reduced to its simpler subcomponents. The model of classroom dialogue that we have presented does, however, offer several features that makes a task analysis approach feasible.

As noted earlier, a central feature of task analysis is the identification of a hierarchy of complexity. In the model developed here, two such hierarchies have been identified. They correspond to the roles played by each of the participants in the Dialogue. On the one hand, there is the increasingly complex range of demands that may be posed by the teacher (i.e., the Group I to IV demands). On the other hand, there is the adequacy of responses that may be offered by the child (i.e., from No Response to Fully Adequate responses). By merging these two hierarchies of behavior, it becomes possible to employ a task-analysis type of approach that may ultimately serve to enhance the child's discourse skills. The major elements of this approach have been derived from a tutorially based teaching program designed to improve the language functioning of preschool-age children who are likely to fail in school. The principles and techniques of the program are described in detail in a number of publications (Blank, 1972, 1973; Blank et al., 1972; Blank & Solomon, 1968, 1969).

The principle of teaching children what they do not know serves to define the curriculum. Any set of discourse demands that receives less than Fully Adequate responses in either the test or teaching situation can be taken to represent an area of discourse that the children have not yet mastered. Accordingly, it also represents an area that can, and eventually should, be taught.

The teaching that occurs is based on a feature of dialogue which has not yet been discussed but is critical to the meaningful use of language. Naturally occurring dialogue contains numerous implicit references, that is, ideas that are essential to the topic under discussion but are never stated explicitly and must be inferred by the listener. If someone says, for example, *I saw John yesterday and he is feeling much better,* it is implied that John had been ill or out of sorts. (See Trabasso et al., 1977, for an analysis of the role of inference in the processing of language.) As discourse demands increase in abstraction, the implicit connections become simultaneously more important and less easy to discern. For example, a statement at the level I type of exchange such as *this is a pen,* will pose little difficulty with regard to the issue of implicit references. The object under discussion is clear, and the verbalization maps almost directly onto the object. In contrast, numerous implicit connections exist in a statement from a level IV type of exchange such as, *Lisa didn't get wet even though it was raining hard.* It is implied that Lisa was outside because otherwise her not getting wet would be of little note. It is also implied that she was somehow protected from the rain, but the means for this protection are not (yet) stated.

Adults are so accustomed to automatically making the connections implied in verbal statements that they often fail to see the difficulties that this demand poses for children who are first learning discourse. In our experience, this is a major source of their problems (although, as discussed in Chapter 5, it is not possible to know if their failure is in the area of being unaware of the implicit information or in being unable to express this awareness). Regardless of the source of their difficulties, it appears that a key factor in enhancing discourse skill is to simplify the task in a way that makes explicit for the child the implicit references underlying the exchange.

A Sample Simplification Sequence

The process of making the implicit explicit can be illustrated through the example that was raised in the preceding chapter about the two cups, one with and one without a bottom. As noted there, a child may have selected the appropriate cup, but then have been unable to justify the choice (that is, the child could not answer the question, *why did you pick this one*). At this point, a simplification sequence would begin that might proceed as follows.

Teacher:	Well, why didn't you pick this one? *(referring to the cup without a bottom)*	Group IV: explaining the obstacles to an action
Child:	*(shrugs.)*	
Teacher:	Well, let's try this cup. *(referring to the cup without the bottom)* Go ahead and pour the juice in here.	Group I: following a direction[2]
Child:	*(completes the action)*	
Teacher:	Oh, what happened to the juice?	Group I: naming an action
Child:	It dropped here. *(pointing to the table)*	
Teacher:	That's right. This isn't a good cup to use. Let's try the other one.	Group I: following a direction
Child:	*(pours the juice in the cup with the bottom)*	
Teacher:	Did that work?	Group II: concepts: identifying characteristics
Child:	*(nods)*	
Teacher:	Let's look at these cups. Look, this one worked and this didn't. What's the difference between these cups? *(holds both cups in front of the child)*	Group II: concepts: identifying differences
Child:	It's got a hole. *(pointing to the cup without the bottom)*	

---

[2]This demand, that is, following a direction, like other demands in actual lessons, is not identical to the items in the test. This is inevitable since the test could not possibly cover every type of demand that can be asked of a young child. Demands that are not included in the test but occur in the dialogue are placed into one of the four groupings. The placement of these demands is carried out in accord with the definitions of the various groups as outlined in Chapter 3 (e.g., if a demand requires the level of abstraction characteristic of Group I items, it is placed in Group I; if it requires the level of abstraction characteristic of Group II items, it is placed in Group II, and so on).

Teacher:	Right. So why shouldn't we use this cup?	Group IV: explaining the obstacles to an action
Child:	It's got a hole.	
Teacher:	And why should we use this cup? *(referring to the cup with the bottom)*	Group IV: explaining the means to a goal
Child:	It don't got no holes.	

Before examining the simplification sequence, it is important to point out that the last question in the sequence represents a rephrasing of the original question, in either identical or nearly identical form. The aim is not simply to have the children answer the question appropriately. It is hoped that the sequence has also provided them with a model whereby they can identify the information needed for this type of problem. (The child in this example may have realized that an explanation of the inappropriate can be achieved by describing the unusual or malfunctioning characteristic.)

While the first and last questions in this sequence are alike, most other demands in the sequence are at a level of complexity that is lower than the demand that was originally failed. Efforts to make the implicit explicit entail this reduction, for simpler demands are the ones that can focus the child on the relevant but until now implicit information. We have attempted to illustrate this phenomenon by labeling each demand in the simplification sequence according to the label it had in the test. As can be seen there, none of the demands in that sequence is equal in difficulty to the original question.

Simplification Techniques

The posing of simpler problems can be achieved in two ways. First, one can make an easier demand within the same group of discourse skills. An instance of this can be found in the teacher's asking, *why* shouldn't *we use this cup* (referring to the cup without the bottom) after the child has failed *why* should *we use this cup* (referring to the cup with the bottom). Generally, it is easier to explain the inappropriate—that is, to say what is wrong—than it is to explain the appropriate—that is, to say what is right. Thus, although the first simplification is from the same group of demands, it represents a somewhat easier demand. (See Appendix C for an illustration of the way in which demands in each group of skills progress in order of difficulty.)

The second way in which the discourse demand can be reduced is by presenting a problem from a lower group of discourse skills. All the remaining simplification requests in the previous sequence reflect this approach, for none of them go beyond the Group II type demands. The reduction in the difficulty of a demand is not confined to a reduction in the verbal formulation put to the child. Frequently, the material that is accompanying the demand is restructured to focus the child on the relevant but implicit information. For instance, the teacher may ask, "Why does the ball roll?" To this, the child may reply, "'Cause it's red." At this point, the teacher may introduce a red cube and say, "Look, this is red, but see, it doesn't roll. So why does this roll *(pointing to the ball)* and not this?" Here, even though the question that the child failed is essentially repeated, it is now asked in a context in which shape (the dimension that is relevant to this problem) has been highlighted.

Considerable skill is required to recognize precisely how the demand and the material should be altered if the child is to be helped over his or her difficulty. For instance, imagine that in the preceding example, when the child said, *cause it's red,* the teacher elected not to introduce the cube but instead chose to follow up the child's attention to color. This could be done by showing a blue ball and rolling it and then asking, *does a ball have to be red to roll.* In terms of the principles that we have been discussing, this apparent simplification is inappropriate since it does not focus the child on the dimension that is relevant to this problem. Instead, it represents an effort in which the irrelevant information that has already misled the child is made even more central (i.e., the child now sees two balls whose distinctive difference is in the dimension of color). As a result, while this approach seems to follow the child's lead, it may actually serve only to exacerbate the preschooler's problems with the irrelevant.

The principles discussed here place restrictions on what the teacher may do after diagnosing (either through test results or classroom exchange) the type of discourse demands that pose difficulties for the child. The questions asked in the simplification effort, however, can still vary considerably. Almost any question may be asked for the purposes of simplification as long as it represents a somewhat easier demand and as long as its content is focused on the implicit but relevant information.[3] In an effort to capture the patterns that underlie successful simplifications, a set of rules has been formulated that has been termed *simplification techniques* (Blank, 1972; Blank, 1977).

Table 6-1 lists the major simplification techniques that are applicable to

---

[3]Occasionally, the identical demand that was failed may be repeated with no intervening simpler questions. This occurs most commonly when the child is inattentive and has simply not listened to the request. Even here, however, the repetition is frequently marked by a different tone or stress that eases the task by helping to focus the child's attention (see Table 6-1).

Table 6-1 *Simplification Techniques for the Management of Nonadequate Responses*

1. **Delay**
   Sample problem: Teacher says, "Pick up the. . . ." Child starts grabbing objects.
   Simplification: Teacher says, "Wait a minute. Listen to what I want you to pick up."

2. **Focus for attention**
   Sample problem: Teacher says, "Go to the sink and get me the pot." Child goes to the sink and reaches for the first thing she or he sees, which is a glass.
   Simplification: Teacher asks, "Do you remember what I asked you to bring?"

3. **Repeats demand**
   Sample problem: Teacher says, "Put your coat on the chair next to the table." Child puts the coat on the table.
   Simplification: Teachers says, "No, not on the table. Put it on the chair that's next to the table."

4. **Synonomous rephrasing**
   Sample problem: Teacher says, "Lift the box off the floor." Child does nothing.
   Simplification: Teacher says, "I mean I want you to pick it up with your hands."

5. **Partially completes task**
   Sample problem: Teacher asks, "What is a pail for?" Child says nothing.
   Simplification: Teacher says, "It can carry w_____."

6. **Restructures task to highlight specific components**
   Sample problem: Teacher asks, "Why do you think we couldn't get this sponge into the [too small] cup and we could fit the marble?" Child says, "Because it's a sponge."
   Simplification: Teacher says, "Okay, I'll cut this sponge into two. Now it's still a sponge. Why does it go into the cup now?"

7. **Offers relevant comparisons**
   Sample problem: Teacher asks, "Where did the ball go?" Child says nothing.
   Simplification: Teacher says, "Well, let's see. Did it go under the table or did it go under the chair?"

8. **Didactic presentation of information**
   Sample problem: Teacher asks, "Could you go over there and get me the strainer?" Child goes to table and looks bewildered.
   Simplification: Teacher asks, "Do you know what a strainer is?" Child shakes head. Teacher says, "Look, this one is a strainer."

9. **Relating unknown to known**
   Sample problem: Teacher says, "Now the spaghetti is hard. How do you think it will feel after it is cooked?" Child says, "I don't know."
   Simplification: Teacher asks, "Well, do you remember when we cooked the potatoes? How did they feel?"

Table 6-1 *(continued)*

---

10. Directed action to recognize salient characteristics
  Sample problem: Teacher asks, "How is the ice different from the water?"
  Child says, "I don't know."
  Simplification: Teacher says, "Well let's see. Turn over the cup of water and
  turn over the tray of ice.

11. Focus on relevant features
  Sample problem: Teacher asks, "Why did you pull your hand away from the
  stove?" Child says nothing.
  Simplification: Teacher asks, "Well, how did the stove feel?"

---

the young child. Each of these techniques can be applied to any level of cognitive demand. For example, one technique, number 7, is termed *Offers Relevant Comparisons.* This can be used if a child offers an Inadequate response to a Group I demand; for example, if a child does not answer when he or she is shown a cup and asked, *what is this,* the teacher may ask, *well, is it a shoe, a cup, or a book.* Similarly, the technique can be used equally well if the child fails a Group IV demand; for example, if a child has said nothing when asked, *what will happen to a pile of blocks if the bottom one is removed,* the teacher may ask, *will the pile stay on the table or will it fall down.* In other words, the techniques represent the types of restructuring and rephrasing that can be used across demands at all levels of abstraction.

The key to the use of the simplification techniques is not the type of demand that is failed but rather the type of response that is offered. That is, one set of techniques is useful for an Invalid response, another for an Associated response, another for an I Don't Know response, and so on. For instance, in both examples here (naming the cup and predicting about the blocks), the child said nothing. With this sort of response, the technique of *Offering Relevant Comparisons* is often helpful. If the child's response had been different, however, this technique might well have been inappropriate. For example, if the child had said *coffee* in response to cup, it might have been disconcerting if the teacher's reply had been, *is it a cup or a book.* The presentation of comparisons or alternatives in this situation is tantamount to acting as if the child had never offered any response. Rather than presenting alternatives, therefore, it would have been far more appropriate for the teacher to use the technique of *Didactic Presentation of Information* (e.g., "Yes, we drink coffee from this. But that's not its name. It is called a cup"). The teacher could then conclude the sequence by saying, "Now, you say 'cup.'" The request to imitate the word *cup* represents a simple demand (Group I: imitation); nevertheless, it is a demand that tests the child's attention to the information that has been offered. In addition, it meets the major criterion for the effective use of simplification techniques: it has made explicit the information needed to meet the initial demand that was posed.

The issue of matching the simplification technique to the quality of the child's response is complex and best illustrated through actual examples of teacher–child interaction. Relevant examples are shown in Table 6-2, in which a number of possible responses have been offered to the single demand: *what will happen to the scale if I put another one here* (referring to a weight and pointing to one side). (This is a Group IV demand: predicting: changes in structure.) The techniques offered do not cover all of the possible ways in which each response could be treated. They are designed solely to illustrate the ways in which responses may be handled by the teacher. For all types of responses except two, simplification techniques are offered to show how the child's answer might be dealt with. The major exception is the Irrelevant response. In our experience, most Irrelevant responses indicate that the problem is so far beyond the child's level (at the moment at least) that any attempt to pursue it will only lead to confusion and frustration for both teacher and child. Such failures, therefore, can be used only as signs of what the child should *not* be taught. We also do not treat acceptable–extraneous responses with simplification. Any effort at simplification would only focus the child on the irrelevant information. Instead, the extraneous information is ignored and the correct part of the child's response is reinforced by the teacher.

The approach outlined here represents our method of helping children develop competencies once their areas of weakness have been diagnosed. We have found it to be a valuable approach for teaching young children, but it is still in its initial stages of development. We offer it at this time not as a complete and final product, but rather as a means for demonstrating the way in which the analysis of discourse may be used to foster higher levels of functioning in children.

ACCOMMODATION TO DIFFERENT SKILLS

We now shift our attention from the strategy of Developing Competence to the stragegy of Accommodation to Different Skills. With this shift, our efforts are refocused from concentrating on what the child does not know to concentrating on what she or he does know. This entails changes in the

Table 6-2   Matching the Simplification Techniques to the Child's Level of Response

Sample Task: Child is shown a toy balance scale containing weights on each side. The adults hold up a small weight and asks, "Why will happen to the scale if I put another one here?" *(pointing to one side)*

Type of Response	Example of Child's Response	Simplified Request	Type of Simplification
Acceptable: Imprecise	*(Pointing)* Down.	That's right. (a) It will go down. (b) You say that.	a. didactic presentation b. focus for attention
Acceptable: Oblique	There'll be another thing in the cup.	That's right. There'll be another thing in the cup. But *which way* will it move?	focus on relevant features
Acceptable: Extraneous	It will go down 'cos it's white.	That's right. It will go down.	(No simplification is used—the extraneous information is ignored)
Ambiguous	It'll move.	Show me *which way* it will move.	focus on relevant features
Inadequate: Invalid	It will go up.	Well. (a) Let's try it and see. (b) Which way did it go?	a. directed action b. focus on relevant features
Inadequate: Associated	It's red.	But watch. (a) It's going to move when I put this in. (b) Now, which way did it move?	a. didactic presentation b. focus on relevant features
Inadequate: Irrelevant	I got one at home.	——	no simplification is used
Inadequate: I Don't Know	I don't know what'll happen.	Do you remember what happened when you put the doll on the [toy] see-saw?	relating unknown to known
Inadequate: No Response	*(shrugs)*	(a) Let's do it. (b) Show me which side went down.	a. directed action b. focus on relevant features

curriculum that will be offered to the child. When the strategy is one of Developing Competence, the core of the teaching is the discourse skills themselves. By contrast, when the strategy is Accommodation to Different Skills, the goal is to use whatever discourse skill the child possesses as a means of engaging him or her in appealing and informative material. Relevant materials might involve stories, arts and crafts, lessons, or trips that the class has taken. In all cases, the focus is on the experience being considered. Discourse is no longer at the center of the stage. It has reverted to its more usual role of being the unnoticed medium of exchange. Nevertheless, it continues to exert a vital influence, for if the subject matter under discussion is to be understood by the child, it must be presented within the child's already existing range of discourse skills.

In order to illustrate the constraints that are present, let us imagine that there is a lesson on transportation in which the teacher wants the children to compare the relative advantages and disadvantages of a car and a bicycle. If the children have mastered Group I and II skills, it is then possible to impose demands such as, *which one has more wheels, find another thing we ride in that has wheels, what do we do with a car,* and *what do we do with a bicycle.* On the other hand, unless the children have mastered Group III and IV skills, it is frustrating and ultimately counterproductive to ask questions such as, *what is the same about a bicycle and a car, why does the windshield in a car have to be made out of glass instead of metal,* and *tell me what a bicycle is.*

In stating that the children must have mastered Group III and IV skills in order to cope with the latter group of questions, we are referring to the 50 percent criterion. In our experience, if children can cope with the majority of demands in a group, then they will also be able to maintain their interest and not be overwhelmed or frustrated even when some of the demands are ones that they do not fully comprehend.

Restrictions are naturally imposed when one attempts to match the discussion to the child's level since it means that many types of questions must be consciously avoided by the teacher. Nevertheless, as long as the child is willing to relate to an adult and evidences mastery over some range of discourse skills (i.e., Group I skills or Group I and II skills), then productive exchanges are possible. In order to provide an illustration of such an exchange, we have chosen to present a lesson between a teacher and a five-year-old child, Joanna, who evidences limited mastery over the range of discourse skills. Her performance on the test of discourse yields the following four scores: Group I, 2.7; Group II, 2.0; Group III, 1.2; and Group IV, 1.1.

The lesson that follows is designed to require those skills that she has already mastered and basically avoid those demands that she has not yet achieved. This goal means that the dialogue is restricted mainly to Group I and II skills. However, it also includes some of the easier Group III and IV skills that Joanna is just beginning to master. (See Appendix C for the order of difficulty of the different processes within each group of discourse skills.) As in any assessment, there is not a perfect correspondence between performance on the test and performance when similar demands are posed in the classroom setting. However, we have found the correspondence to be quite high with the result that the test performance can be a useful guide to the design of any lesson.

The lesson is carried out in a one-to-one setting because the presence of several children makes it difficult to illustrate the match between the teacher's demands and the child's skills.[4] The content of the lesson is concerned with a nutcracker, an object that attracted Joanna's curiosity when she saw it illustrated in a book.

Early in the lesson, the teacher asks Joanna to pick out some nuts and place them on the table. In the ensuing discussion, Joanna recognizes that the nut shells are hard and cannot be eaten. The teacher then brings the nutcracker over, saying that it is "something that could take the shell off." (The nutcracker is a wooden one with a cup at one end into which the nut can be placed. A wooden screw is then inserted into the cup to crack the nut.) To aid the transition between the test and the teaching, whenever appropriate, each demand in the teaching exchange is in bold and coded according to the group to which it corresponds in the test, and each response of the child is coded as it would be coded in the test situation. As the reader will note, the teacher also uses language that does not involve the imposition of demands. For example, at times she acknowledges the child's behavior (e.g., *that's right*), at other times she praises the child (e.g., *you're doing so well*), and at still other times she prefaces her questions with information that makes the question more meaningful to the child (e.g., *now we will have to make this work so it will break the shells*). The various types of language are important in the discourse and merit consideration in their own right. (Interested readers may refer to Blank, 1977, for a discussion of this component of teacher language.)

The lesson proceeds as follows:

---

[4]While matching of demands to the child's level is more difficult in a group setting, it nevertheless can be achieved. It is, however, difficult to illustrate the matching in a written dialogue. For this reason we have elected to use the one-to-one exchange in the lesson presented here.

		Teacher's Demand	Child's Response
Teacher:	*(holding the nutcracker)* Now, we have to make this work so it will break the shells. Look carefully. There's a part on it that moves. **Look and see if you can find which part moves.**	Group II: identifying an object by function	
Joanna:	*(carefully examines the nutcracker and then points to the stem)*		Fully Adequate
Teacher:	That's right. If you turn it, it will move. **Go ahead and try it.**	Group I: following a direction	
Joanna:	*(turns handle while the teacher holds the nutcracker)*		Fully Adequate
Teacher:	**What happens when you turn this?** *(pointing to the screw)*	Group II: describing an event	
Joanna:	This: *(gestures in a way to indicate that the screw moves into the cup)*		Acceptable: Imprecise
Teacher:	**And what do you think would happen if we put a nut in there?**	Group IV: predicting	
Joanna:	*(says nothing)*		Inadequate: No Response
Teacher:	Well, let's try it and see what happens. Here, **take a nut and put it in.** *(hands Joanna a nut)*	Group I: following a direction	

Joanna:	(takes a nut and puts it into the cup of the nutcracker)		Fully Adequate
Teacher:	Good. **Now go ahead and turn it.**	Group I: following a direction	
Joanna:	(intensely starts to twist the screw)		Fully Adequate
Teacher:	That's hard work. You're doing so well at it. (suddenly there is a cracking sound) Look at the nut. **What happened?**	Group II: describing an event	
Joanna:	It got into pieces.		Fully Adequate
Teacher:	**Which part broke into pieces?**	Group II: identifying attributes	
Joanna:	The nut.		Ambiguous
Teacher:	**Was it the shell or was it the part we could eat?**	Group II: identifying attributes	
Joanna:	The shell.		Fully Adequate
Teacher:	Very good. Now that the shell is off, we can eat it. **But how are we going to get the nut out of the nutcracker?** See it's stuck in there so tight. (pulls at the nut to show the child that that nut is stuck)	Group IV: Formulating a solution	
Joanna:	(pulls at the nut)		Inadequate: Irrelevant (Imitating teacher's action)
Teacher:	No, we just won't be able to get it out that way. We have to do something		

	else. Let me show you. *(takes nutcracker and starts turning the handle in the opposite direction)* **What am I doing?**	Group II: describing an event
Joanna:	Like that. *(gestures)*	Acceptable: Imprecise
Teacher:	Yes, I'm going like that I'm turning the handle. **You say that.**	Group I: imitating a simple sentence
Joanna:	Turning the handle.	Acceptable: Imprecise
Teacher:	That's right—I'm turning the handle. And **now will we be able to take the nut out?**	Group IV predicting: yes–no
Joanna:	*(nods)*	Ambiguous[5]
Teacher:	Okay, **take it out, put the shell in this cup,** and **put the part that we can eat on this plate.**	Group III: following a set of directions
Joanna:	*(puts both the shell and the meat of the nut on the plate)*	Ambiguous
Teacher:	Yes, I wanted this *(pointing to the meat of the nut)* on the plate, but I didn't want the	

---

[5]With a yes–no demand, it is difficult to evaluate the child's response since there is a 50 percent likelihood of an Adequate response by chance alone. Accordingly the response is placed in the Ambiguous category. This procedure is not designed or used to serve as a handicap to the child. Rather, it is used mainly to keep the teacher aware of the fact that such questions by themselves do not yield much information about the child's discourse skill.

	shells there. We can't eat the shell so I wanted it on a a different plate. **Here, put the shell in this cup.**	Group I: following a direction
Joanna:	*(does it)*	Fully Adequate
Teacher:	That's very good. Now we're going to eat this part. *(pointing to the meat of nut)* But before we do, let me ask you something. **Do you remember the name of the thing we used to break the nut open?**	Group II: recalling information
Joanna:	*(no response)*	Inadequate: No Response
Teacher:	Let me see. **Do you think it's called an apple-cracker or a nutcracker?**	Group II: recalling information
Joanna:	Nutcracker.	Fully Adequate
Teacher:	That's right and **next time that you want to crack some nuts and you want to use my nutcracker, what will you say to me?**	Group III: assuming a role
Joanna:	Give me the nutcracker.	Fully Adequate
Teacher:	That's really fine.	

The preceding dialogue represents only about half of the lesson between the teacher and Joanna. In the later unreported part of the lesson, Joanna is asked to draw the nutcracker. In general, her drawing skills are quite good and so this activity leads her to focus much more attentively on the actual construction of the object. In addition, the drawing activity is guided by questions and demands from the teacher that extend and enhance the earlier exchange (e.g., requests are made such as *show me the part you're going to draw now, how many parts are there in this nut-cracker,* and *what shape did you make the cup of the nutcracker*).

Regardless of the changing emphasis in the lesson, however, the overall lesson is characterized by a single, dominating theme; that is, the demands are confined to the range of discourse skills that have been diagnosed through the test as being in the child's repertoire.[6]

THE IDEAL: A BLEND

Up to this point, the positions of Developing Competence and Accommodation to Different Skills have been presented as mutually exclusive alternatives. While this opposition is useful for purposes of exposition, in actual practice the two approaches need not be independent. Indeed, a blend of the two is not only possible, it is generally highly desirable. The sphere of discourse is particularly suited to such a blend since language plays complementary roles in each alternative; that is, in Developing Competence, language is the *content* of the exchange, while in Accommodation to Different Skills, language is the *medium* of the exchange.

The blending of the two approaches can be seen to some degree in the lesson with Joanna. Blending is intentionally downplayed in that lesson since its aim is to highlight the way in which a subject matter can be discussed productively even when one remains within a relatively limited discourse range. Nevertheless, Joanna still gives evidence that some of the demands posed are not yet firm in her repertoire (e.g., in reply to, *what do you think would happen if we put a nut in there,* she says nothing). At these points, the teacher initiates some brief simplification sequences to help the child understand the information that is asked in the question.

Had the lesson been designed to Develop Competence in discourse, more complex demands would have been posed, and longer, more intricate simplification sequences would have been initiated. The exact balance in the relationship between a Development strategy and an Accommodation strategy remains to be determined. In our experience in dealing with preschool-age children who have difficulties in the sphere of dis-

---

[6]The discussion here has focused on techniques that might be introduced to make the preschool experience fruitful for children with limited discourse skills. As is clear by its absence, no consideration has been given to alternative approaches that might be used to facilitate the child's functioning (e.g., parent training). While these alternative approaches represent potentially important avenues for change, it is crucial to recognize that they too involve the realm of verbal communication. As a result, many of the issues discussed here may be applicable to these programs as well.

course, the most effective balance seems to be about 70 percent Accommodation to Different Skills and about 30 percent Development of Competence; that is to say most of the time the dialogue should remain within the range that the children have already mastered, while for about one-third of the time, the dialogue should go on to demands that the children have not yet attained. The high percentage of discourse that remains within children's already available skills serves several purposes. First, it allows the children to feel successful in the exchange with the teacher; second, it permits them a chance to rehearse their skills and extend their use to new situations; third, it affords them an opportunity to understand most of the material being discussed, thereby allowing them to extend their general knowledge and information. In this predominantly successful and interesting setting, the children are then willing and able to deal with the more complex discourse demands that they have not yet mastered. The degree to which they will profit from these new demands depends in major part on the success with which the teacher is able to offer carefully detailed simplification sequences.

A number of considerations, other than relative percentages, determine the effectiveness of a Development–Accommodation blend. For example, it is difficult to begin intricate simplification sequences at the end of a lesson when the child is tired. As a result, it is preferable to present the more complex discourse demands in the first half of a lesson, for these are the demands that are likely to elicit Inadequate responses and, hence, lead to long simplification sequences. The set of principles that governs a successful Accommodation–Development blend is discussed in Blank (1973). At this time, we have simply tried to highlight the ways in which the information available in the model and the test may be applied to enhance the teacher–child exchange.

SUMMARY

This chapter has been devoted to considering the implications that the test results hold for the feasibility of preschool education. In line with current reformulations of the school's roles and responsibilities, it seems that our findings can be used profitably in accord with two different models of schooling. In one model, the Development of Initial Competence, the emphasis is on helping the child develop mastery of areas in which he or she is weak. When this approach is applied to the sphere of discourse, the idea that emerges is the enhancement of the child's skill in order to permit her or him to understand the full range of demands that occur in teacher–child exchange. The critical yardsticks for aiding the child are the type of demand and the quality of the response. Any type of demand that systematically leads to other than Fully Adequate responses represents a potential area in which the child's behavior can be fostered. It has further been suggested that effective fostering of a child's behavior depends on the use of simplification techniques, that is, on the use of techniques whereby the initial demand is reduced or simplified so that the child is led to recognize the essential but implicit information that is necessary for an Adequate response to that demand.

In a second model of schooling, Accommodation to Different Skills, the emphasis is on the need for the school to adapt to the skills that the children possess, rather than to those that they lack. When this approach is combined with our analysis of discourse, it appears that the teacher's demands should be confined to those processes of discourse that the child's performance demonstrates that he or she has already mastered. An illustration of this approach is offered in a dialogue between a teacher and a five-year-old child. Although the discourse demands are restricted, the subject matter is not. Any subject matter that arouses the child's interest and motivation can serve as the core of the discussion.

Although the two models of schooling have been presented as alternatives, in actual practice it is not only feasible, but highly desirable to combine them within any teacher–child exchange, since different functions are served by dialogue within each model. In the Development of Competence model, dialogue skills are enhanced. In the Accommodation model, dialogue skills become the medium for enhancing the child's general fund of knowledge. When blended, the two approaches, therefore, serve complementary roles in which an optimal teacher–child exchange may be achieved.

A Concluding Statement

Because language is such a remarkably flexible and versatile tool, it has been studied by a number of disciplines, each of which has interpreted it somewhat differently. Thus, in linguistics language is divided into categories such as lexicon, syntax, and phonology; in psychology it is divided into categories such as concepts, labeling, and problem solving; while in neurology there are groupings such as sequencing and expressive versus receptive language.

Over the years, these various ideas have filtered their way into education and have determined, in large measure, the way in which language is assessed and taught in the schools. The influence of these disparate approaches is reflected in the partitioning of language curricula into categories that are nearly identical to the rubrics of academic research. Thus, a portion of the school day may be devoted to the teaching of concepts, another to the expansion of grammatical structures, and still another to the enhancement of sequencing skills. This division is clearly useful for research purposes. In any instance of real language, however, all of the elements will be present simultaneously. Hence, the use of compartmentalized units in the classroom may well violate essential elements of natural language functioning and be of questionable value in helping children use language more effectively.

Education's reliance on academic disciplines for the development of language curricula, however, has led to an even greater problem. In most analyses of language, relatively little attention has been devoted to the role of communication. Since education borrows heavily from these analyses, the neglect of communication in research studies on language is mirrored by a comparable neglect in the development of curricula for the classroom setting. As a result, there is pitifully little known about language in its role as the essential and invaluable medium of exchange between the teacher and the child.

The communication aspect of language requires the consideration of a host of ideas not commonly raised when language is analyzed according to such traditional rubrics as lexicon, concepts, and the like. The work that is presented here has been designed to deal with some of the issues that we believe must be considered if there is to be a coherent picture of language as a tool of communication between the teacher and the child. To this end we have:

1. created a model that encompasses the language teachers must use when engaging in discourse with children
2. devised a test to assess the degree to which young children possess mastery of these discourse skills
3. examined the patterns of performance that young children display
4. presented ways in which the instructional process may be modified in order to take account of the child's level of proficiency in discourse

Given the complexity of the issues and the state of knowledge in each, it is clear that the work that has been presented should be seen as a preliminary foray into an intricate domain. As the research progresses, each of the issues we have considered will almost certainly require modification and elaboration. In addition, many other areas must ultimately be included if we are to have a full understanding of the language of instruction. For example (to cite but a few), consideration must be given to the ways in which (1) the various requests and ideas must be sequenced if the child is to follow the full scope of any discussion, (2) the language must be varied so that the teacher does not begin to rely on a rote, predictable, and uninteresting dialogue, and (3) the child's spontaneous comments may be productively incorporated into the teaching exchange.

We have only begun to scratch the surface of the many complex processes that underlie effective language exchange. We do hope, however, that the work we have presented can provide productive guidelines for continued research in this vital area. It is in this spirit that we offer this book to the reader.

The work described so far has been based on the lengthy and comprehensive test of discourse skills (described in Chapter 3). While it is possible to use this type of test for research purposes, it is not practical for everyday use in the school setting. Because there is often a need to assess young children's language abilities, particularly in the realm of communication, a shortened and modified experimental version of the discourse test—the Preschool Language Assessment Instrument (PLAI)—has been developed. This test is presented in a companion volume to this book, called Preschool Language Assessment Instrument: The Language of Learning in Practice, *which is written by us and published by Grune & Stratton. PLAI requires about 20 minutes to administer and is designed to be given in a one-to-one testing situation. It is strongly urged that the test be used only by those who are fully acquainted with the material and ideas presented here since these concepts are essential to a meaningful interpretation of any child's performance.*

Appendixes

Appendix A

The Test in Detail

This appendix outlines each of the demands in the test. As described in Chapter 3, the test is designed to represent four major categories of demands, termed: I, Matching Perception; II, Selective Analysis of Perception; III, Reordering Perception; and IV, Reasoning about Perception. In turn, each of the major groupings involves a series of different processes. For example, Group I, Matching Perception, covers processes such as naming objects, matching objects, and recalling information. Each process is assessed by several items, varying generally from two to six in number. In the description that follows, each of these related items is referred to as a "cluster." Because of limited space, only one item—the sample item—from each cluster is outlined in detail. The remaining items are outlined as well, but in less detail. In all cases, they follow the format of the sample item. Although the items are presented in sequence, from Group I to Group IV, in the actual administration of the test the items from all the groups are interspersed with one another. Occasionally, notes are presented after the description of certain items to explain how the particular item under discussion relates to other items in the test or to elaborate on some specific information that is relevant to that item. The remainder of Appendix A will be devoted to a description of the test items.

GROUP I: MATCHING PERCEPTION

The following clusters of items tap the demands in this group:

A. Scanning for a matching object *(Find one like this).*
B. Identifying an object by sound *(Show me what you heard.)*
C. Identifying an object by touch *(Show me what you touched).*
D. Naming an object heard *(What did you hear?)*

E. Naming an object touched *(What did you touch?)*
F. Naming an object seen *(What is this?)*
G. Imitating a simple sentence *(Say this . . .)*
H. Remembering pictured objects *(What did you see?)*
I. Remembering incidental information *(What did you see?)*

The specific items in each cluster area are as follows.

A. Scanning for a matching object
    total number in cluster: 4
1. sample item
Material   consists of a paring knife and a large oak tag card containing 20 pictures of common objects. One of the pictures is a duplicate of the knife shown, but several of the items pictured are similar in shape or function to the knife (e.g., scissors), and some are associated with the context in which the knife is used (e.g., food).
Task   tester holds up the knife and says, "Look at this. When I show you the card, I want you to point to one like it." Tester removes the knife from view and places the card in front of the child, saying, "Now point to it." (If the child does not respond within 15 seconds, the request is repeated.)
(See Appendix B, p. 161, for scoring.)
   Other items in this cluster are:
2. matching a crayon
3. matching a wire clothes hanger
4. matching a frying pan
(different cards are used for each item)

B. Identifying an object by sound
    total number in cluster: 3
1. sample item
Material   consists of a bell and a wooden board containing a whistle, a bell, a harmonica, and a rattle.
Task   tester says, "Turn around and don't look, just listen." The bell is then rung three times out of the child's view. The bell is put away, the child is asked to turn back, the board is shown to the child, and the tester asks, "Which one of these things made that noise?"
(See Appendix B, p. 162, for scoring.)
   Other items in this cluster involve identification of:
2. a zipper, with the array composed of a gun, a hammer, a zipper, and scissors
3. a set of keys, with the array composed of keys, a rattle, an egg beater, and a xylophone

C. Identifying an object by touch
    total number in cluster: 3

1. sample item
Material   consists of a rubber ball and a wooden board containing a ball, a yo-yo, a styrofoam disc, and a wax pear.
Task   tester says, "Turn around and put your hands behind your back because I want you to feel something." The ball is placed in the child's hands, and she or he is told, "Feel it all over." (If child fails to do so, the tester moves the child's hands around the ball.) The ball is put away, the child is asked to turn back, the board is shown to the child, and the tester asks, "Which one of these things were you just holding?"
(See Appendix B, p. 162, for scoring.)
   Other items in this cluster involve identification of:
2.   a teaspoon, with the array composed of a knife, a fork, a tea strainer, and a teaspoon
3.   a baby's shoe, with the array composed of a mitten, a change purse, a furry slipper, and a baby's shoe

D. Naming an object heard
      total number in cluster: 3
1.   sample item
Material   consists of the array from the sample item in I-B.
Task   after the child has selected an item in the array in I-B, the array is removed, and the tester asks, "What was the name of the thing that made that noise?"
(See Appendix B, p. 139, for scoring.)
   Other items in this cluster involve:
2.   labeling a zipper, from I-B (second item)
3.   labeling a set of keys, from I-B (third item)

E. Naming an object touched
      total number in cluster: 3
1.   sample item
Material   consists of the array from the sample item in I-C.
Task   after the child has selected an item in the array in I-C, the array is removed and tester asks, "What was the name of the thing that you were just holding?"
(See Appendix B, p. 139, for scoring.)
   Other items in this cluster involve:
2.   labeling a teaspoon, from I-C (second item)
3.   labeling a shoe, from I-C (third item)

F. Naming an object seen
      total number in cluster: 3

1. sample item
Material consists of a small blue toy car.
Task tester shows the car to the child and asks, "What is this called?"
(See Appendix B, p. 139, for scoring.)
   Other items in this cluster are:
2. labeling a pair of scissors
3. labeling a cup

G. Imitating a simple sentence
   total number in cluster: 6
1. sample item
Material none.
Task tester says, "You say what I say: *'The ball was in the house.'*"
(See Appendix B, p. 140, for scoring.)
   Other items in this cluster require the child to imitate the following sentences:
2. The boy saw the dog.
3. The teacher read the story.
4. The girl looked out the window.
5. The boy played with the ball.
6. The car went down the street.

H. Remembering pictured objects
   total number in cluster: 4
1. sample item
Material consists of an oak tag card containing five pictures of common objects (carriage, coat, kettle, toaster, flower).
Task tester says, "I'm going to show you a card with some pictures." The card is displayed and the tester adds, "Look at them carefully because I am going to take them away soon." After five seconds, the card is turned over and the tester asks, "What things did you see there?"
(See Appendix B, p. 141, for scoring.)
   Other items in this cluster involve:
2. Card with 15 items (bookcase, iron, jacket, trash can, bell, milk truck, toothbrush, carriage, traffic light, pencil, scissors, dress, piggy bank, sink, pot). Instructions are the same as in H1
3. Card with 5 items (bird, book, sweater, package, screwdriver). The instructions are less focused than in the first two items in that the request for attention is less explicit. Specifically, the child is told only, "Here, look at these pictures."
4. Card with 15 items (coffee pot, airplane, apples, house, clock, crib, truck, hen, cake, drum, knife, car, pocketbook, glass, zipper). The instructions are the same as in the preceding item.

I. Remembering incidental information
   total number in cluster: 5
1. sample item
Material consists of five small boxes, each displaying one of the following pictures—spoon, book, ball, apple, and pencil—and a set of wooden squares, each displaying one of the same pictures.
Task tester points to the squares and says, "Put each of these things into the box that has the same picture." When this is completed, the pictures are turned away so that they are out of the child's sight. The tester then asks, "What pictures did you just put into the boxes?"
(See Appendix B, p. 141, for scoring.)
   Other items in this cluster involve:
2. recalling the names of pictures in matching task involving blocks, shoes, cat, bicycle, and crib
3. recalling the pictures in one of the scanning tasks in I-A, that is, after the card is withdrawn, the child is asked, "What else did you see on that card?"
4. recalling the objects on the board in the auditory task in I-B, that is, after the board is withdrawn, the child is asked, "What else did you see there?"
5. recalling the objects on the board in the tactual task in I-C, that is, after the board is withdrawn, the child is asked, "What else did you see there?"

GROUP II: SELECTIVE ANALYSIS OF PERCEPTION

The demands in this group are tapped by the following clusters of items:

A. Scanning for an object defined by its function *(Find one that can. . . .)*
B. Describing a scene *(What is happening?)*
C. Recalling items named in a statement *(What things . . .?)*
D. Recalling information from a statement *(Who? What? Where?)*
E. Completing a sentence *(Finish this . . . .)*
F. Concepts: Naming characteristics and functions of objects *(Tell me its . . . .)*
G. Concepts: Attending to two characteristics *(Find the one that is . . . and. . . .)*
H. Concepts: Identifying differences *(How are these different?)*
I. Concepts: Citing an example within a category *(Name something that is a. . . .)*

   The specific items in each cluster are as follows.
A. Scanning for an object defined by its function
   total number in cluster: 4

1.   sample item
Material[1]   consists of a large oak tag card containing 20 pictures of common objects, including a knife.
Task   tester says, "When I show you the card I want you to find me something we could cut with."
(See Appendix B, p. 161, for scoring.)
   Other items in this cluster require the child to
2.   find something we could color with
3.   find something we could hang a dress on
4.   find something we could cook with
(different cards are used for each item)

B. Describing a scene
      total number in cluster: 2
1.   sample item
Material   consists of a picture of a girl playing with a doll at a table set for a meal.
Task   the picture is shown and the tester asks, "What's happening in the picture now?"
(See Appendix B, p. 142, for scoring.)
   The other item in this cluster involves:
2.   a picture of a boy riding a bike. The same question is asked as in the preceding (sample) item.

C. Recalling items named in a statement
      total number in cluster: 2
1.   sample item
Material   consists of a closed book.
Task   tester says, "I'm going to show you a picture of a cat and a lady."
Tester picks book up and says, "Before I open this, what did I say I was going to show you?"
(See Appendix B, p. 143, for scoring.)
   The other item in this cluster is as follows:
2.   the tester says, "The other day I bought milk, crayons, and a newspaper when I went to the store to do my shopping. What things did I say I bought when I went shopping?"

D. Recalling information from a statement
      total number in cluster: 6

------

[1]The material in all the items in this cluster is the same as that used in the Group I cluster scanning for a matching object.

1. sample item
Material none.
Task tester says, "I'm going to tell you part of a story. The story starts like this: 'James and Ann walked down the street to see their friend's new car.'"
The tester then asks, "What were the children's names?" (subject)
2. "Where were they walking?" (location)
3. "What were they going to see?" (purpose)
(See Appendix B, p. 143, for scoring.)
    Other items in this cluster are:
The child is told, "Little Jack Horner sat in a corner eating a Christmas pie." The child is then asked,
4. "Who was in the story?" (subject)
5. "Where was he sitting?" (location)
6. "What was he doing?" (purpose)

E. Completing a sentence
    total number in cluster: 3
1. sample item
Material none.
Task tester offers a demonstration item first by saying, "You finish what I say. Every morning I go to ———."[2] The child is then asked to complete the sentence, "I like to eat some ———."
(See Appendix B, p. 140, for scoring.)
    Other items in this cluster require the child to complete the following sentences:
2. "I draw with a ———."
3. "I like to look at ———."

F. Concepts: Naming characteristics and functions of objects
    total number in cluster: 9
1. sample item
Material consists of a cup.
Task tester shows the cup and asks
"What do we do with this?" (function)
2. "What is this part for?" *(pointing to handle)* (part-whole relationship)
3. "What color is the cup?" (physical attribute)
(See Appendix B, p. 145, for scoring.)
    Other items in this cluster involve:
a pair of scissors. The questions are:

---

[2]If the child has difficulty, the tester offers an answer"Like I could say, 'Every morning I go to work,' and you could say, 'Every morning I go to ———'").

4. "What do we do with this?" (function);
5. "What is this part for?" *(pointing to the screw in the center)* (part-whole relationship)
6. "What shape is this part?" *(pointing to the opening in the handle)* (physical attribute)

a toy car. The questions are:
7. "What do we do with this?" (function)
8. "What is this part for?" *(pointing to the windshield)* (part-whole relationship)
9. "What shape are the wheels?" (physical attribute)

G. Concepts: Attending to two characteristics
   total number in cluster: 3
1. sample item

Material   consists of a board displaying five cups which are as follows: a large beige cup, upside down, with pictures on the outside; a large beige cup, right side up, with stripes on the outside; a small, yellow cup, upside down, with stripes on the outside; a large beige cup, right side up, with pictures on the outside; and a small, yellow cup, right side up, with no decoration outside.

Task   tester says, "Show me the one that is upside down and has pictures." (See Appendix B, p. 162, for scoring.)

   Other items in this cluster involve:
2. a group of five toy cars differing according to decoration (stripes or flowered decals), color (white, beige, or blue), and style (convertible or sedan). The child is told, "Show me the one that has stripes and a top."
3. a group of five pairs of scissors differing according to size (large or small), color (black, green, or silver handles), and position (open or closed). The child is asked, "Show me the one that is big and opened."

H. Concepts: Identifying differences
   total number in cluster: 4
1. sample item

Material   consists of a board with a scissors and a knife.

Task   tester says, "Look at these. How are they different?" (See Appendix B, p. 146, for scoring.)

   Other items in this cluster require the child to identify the difference between:
2. a bus and a truck
3. two types of candies
4. two types of cups

Note: The materials in this cluster were intentionally chosen so that the objects in two of the sets would share a common label (candy, cup), while the objects in the other two sets would have different labels (scissors––knife; truck–bus). This selection permits an evaluation of whether the presence of similar or different names affects the identification of differences.

I. Concepts: Citing an example within a category
total number in cluster: 4
1. sample item
Material   none.
Task   tester says, "I walked down the street and saw something that had wheels. What could I have seen?"
(See Appendix B, p. 147, for scoring.)
Other items in this cluster are:
2. "A lady washed some clothing. What kind of clothing could she have washed?"
3. "A lady was in the supermarket and saw food. What kind of food could she have seen?"
4. "A little boy went to the zoo and saw an animal. What one could he have seen?"

GROUP III: REORDERING PERCEPTION

The demands in this group are tapped by the following clusters of items:

A. Scanning for an object by integrating verbal with visual information *(Find one to use with this.)*
B. Describing events subsequent to a scene *(What will happen next?)*
C. Assuming the role of another person *(What could . . . say?)*
D. Following a set of directions *(Do this . . . , then this. . . .)*
E. Arranging pictures in a sequence *(Make these into. . . .)*
F. Formulating a set of directions *(Tell me how. . . .)*
G. Formulating a generalization about a set of events *(What happened to all of these?)*
H. Formulating a statement to unify a sequence of pictures *(Tell this story)*
I. Concepts: Identifying similarities *(How are these the same?)*
J. Concepts: Selecting an object by exclusion *(What else . . . ?)*
K. Concepts: Selecting a set of objects by exclusion *(Find the things that are not. . . .)*
L. Concepts: Citing an example by excluding a specific object *(Name something that can . . . but is not a. . . .)*
M. Concepts: Citing an example by excluding a class of objects *(Name something that is not a . . . .)*
N. Concepts: Defining words *(What is a . . . ?)*
?. Unusual imitations *(Say this. . . .)*

The specific items in each cluster are as follows.

A. Scanning for an object by integrating verbal with visual information
total number in cluster: 4

1. sample item

Material[3]   consists of an orange and a large oak tag card containing 20 pictures of common objects, including a paring knife.

Task   tester holds up the orange and says, "When I show you the card I want you to find me something we could cut this with."
(See Appendix B, p. 161, for scoring.)

Other items in this cluster are:

2. Tester holds up a dress and says, "Find something we could hang this on."

3. Tester holds up a paper and says, "Find something I could use to draw on this."

4. Tester holds up an egg and says, "Find something I could cook this in."
(different cards are used for each item)

Note: In all the scanning items of Groups I, II, and III, the correct choice was the same on each card (e.g., the knife as in the sample item just discussed). In Group I, however, the choice was the answer to a visual match (i.e., a knife was held up and the child had to find a comparable picture); in Group II, it was the answer to an object defined by its function (i.e., the request was to find something to cut with); in Group III, it was the answer to an object that would meet the stated requirements of a displayed object (e.g., holding up an orange and saying, *find something to cut this with*). In this way, the visual material and the solution remained the same. Any variation in performance, therefore, could be attributed mainly to variations in the complexity of the instructions.

B. Describing events subsequent to a scene
total number in cluster: 2

1. Sample item

Material[4]   consists of a picture of a girl playing with a doll at a table set for a meal.

Task   tester says, "This girl is playing at the table now. What might she do after she leaves the table?"
(See Appendix B, p. 142, for scoring.)

The other item in this cluster involves:

2. a picture of a boy riding a bicycle. The tester says, "The boy is all finished riding the bicycle. What do you think he might do next?"

---

[3]The material is the same as that used in the Groups I and II clusters scanning for an object.
[4]The material is identical to the material in the task describing a scene in Group II-B.

C. Assuming the role of another person
   total number in cluster: 5
1. sample item
Material consists of a picture of a boy with one shoe off.
Task tester says, "A little boy came to school with only one shoe on."
Tester then asks, "What did the other children say?"
2. "What did the boy say?"
(See Appendix B, p. 148, for scoring.)
   Other items in this cluster involve:
a scene of a man in a garage
The tester says, "I saw a man this morning whose car was broken and he took it to the garage."
3. "What do you think he said to the man in the garage?"
4. "What do you think the man in the garage said to him?"
a picture of a boy, a girl, and a dog
The tester says, "The little girl wants to pat the dog, but the boy is in the way."
5. "If she wants to pat the dog, what should she say to the little boy?"

D. Following a set of directions
   total number in cluster: 2
1. sample item
Material consists of an empty box, a doll wearing clothes, and a doll's hat.
Task tester says, "First, take the socks off the doll, then put the hat in the box, and then put the box on the floor."
(See Appendix B, p. 150, for scoring.)
   The other item in this cluster involves:
2. a book, a pencil, and a sheet of paper
The tester says, "First pick up the pencil, then put it on the book, and then turn over the paper."

E. Arranging pictures in a sequence
   total number in cluster: 3
1. sample item
Material consists of a frame with four partitions and four cards, each with one of the following drawings:
a. a boy reaching toward a bowl of apples on a table
b. the boy next to the table, bringing the apple to his mouth
c. the boy, facing front, opening his mouth (a bite has been taken from the apple)
d. the boy throwing the core into an open trash can
The cards are placed in disarray on the table.

Task   tester says, "These pictures have to be put in here [*pointing to frame*], so that they tell a story about a boy doing something. Now they are not in the right order. They're all mixed up. You fix them and put them in the right order in here. Start here [*pointing to partition on the left*] ."
(See Appendix B, p. 163, for scoring.)
   The other items in this cluster are:
2.   Four pictures, each showing a glass. From one picture to the next, the glass successively has more water.
3.   Four pictures, each containing a leaf and a tree. From one picture to the next, the leaf is falling closer to the ground until, in the last picture, it is on the ground. The instruction and presentation are identical to that of the sample item.

F. Formulating a set of directions
      total number in cluster: 2
1. sample item
Material   consists of Lotto board and cards.
Task   after having matched the cards to the pictures on the Lotto board, the child is asked, "If you wanted to tell your friend how to play this game, what would you say to him [her]?"
(See Appendix B, p. 148, for scoring.)
   The other item in this cluster is,
2.   Following the presentation of an array of objects from the second item in III-J, (described later), the tester says, "See these things. I don't want them on the table anymore. You tell me what I should do with them."

G.   Formulating a generalization about a set of events
      total number in cluster: 3
1. sample item
Material   consists of four glasses of water and jars of red, yellow, green, and blue food coloring.
Task   tester says, "Watch, I'm going to put some of this in here, some of this in here [and so on]." The tester then proceeds to add a different food color to each glass so that the glasses contain either red, yellow, green, or blue water. The tester stirs the colored water (to obtain an even solution) and says, "What happened to the water when I put these things into it?" *(pointing to the jars of food coloring)*
(See Appendix B, p. 151, for scoring.)
   Other items in this cluster involve:
2.   The green colored water in the sample item is removed and the others are mixed (in front of the child) as follows: red and yellow to form orange; blue and yellow to form green, and red and blue to form pur-

ple. In addition, some of each of the original colors is left in each glass. The tester says *(pointing to the original colors),* "What happened when I mixed these together?"

3. Four small glasses are shown, each containing one of the following: soil, pudding, flour, or oatmeal. The tester pours water into each glass and asks, "What happened to these when I added the water?"

H. Formulating a statement to unify a sequence of pictures
   total number in cluster: 2
1. sample item
Material[5] consists of four pictures arranged from left to right, each showing a glass; from one picture to the next, the glass successively has more water, until in the last picture it is filled.
Task the tester says, "Tell me the story of what happened to the glass." (See Appendix B, p. 151, for scoring.)
   The other item in this cluster involves:
2. Four pictures, each containing a leaf and a tree. From one picture to the next, the leaf is falling closer to the ground, until in the last picture it is on the ground. The instructions are the same as in the sample item.

I. Concepts: Identifying similarities
   total number in cluster: 4
1. sample item
Material[6] consists of a board with a scissors and a knife.
Task the tester says, "Look at these. How are they the same?" (See Appendix B, p. 146, for scoring.)
   Other items in this cluster involve:
2. a bus and a truck
3. two types of candies
4. two types of cups
Note: identifying differences was placed in Group II while identifying similarities was placed in Group III. This was done because it was judged that the selection of a feature common to two different objects (the demand in a similarities task) requires a greater reorganization of language and perception than does the identification of two different features present in two different objects (the task required for differences).

---

[5]The material here is the same as that described before in arranging pictures in a sequence (III-E). The task here is given after the child has correctly sequenced the pictures or, failing that, after the tester has arranged the pictures in the correct sequence.
[6]The material in this item, and in all the items in this cluster, is identical to that in identifying differences in II-H.

J. Concepts: Selecting an object by exclusion[7]
   total number in cluster: 2
1. sample item
Material   consists of an array of two identical pencils, a pen, a paintbrush, a bottle of ink, an index card with writing on it, an eraser, and tape.
Task   tester picks up a pencil and asks, "What is this?" After the child responds, the tester replaces the pencil in the array and says, "Now get me something different that writes."
(See Appendix B, p. 152, for scoring.)
   The other item in this cluster involves:
2. an array of two cups, a glass, a bowl, a napkin, a plastic fork, a knife, and a paper plate. The child is asked to label a cup and is then told, "Now get me something different that we drink from."

K. Concepts: Selecting a set of objects by exclusion
   total number in cluster: 4
1. sample item
Material   consists of a casual array of four dolls, a small rubber animal, a ball, and a rattle.
Task   tester says, "Give me the things that are not dolls and tell me when you're finished."
(See Appendix B, p. 152, for scoring.)
   The other items in this cluster involve:
2. A doll next to an array of a cup, a spoon, a ring, a paper plate, rubber pants, a diaper pin, two dolls' shoes, and a small white box. Tester says, "This doll is ready to sleep now. Put away the things she uses when she eats. Put them in here [*points to box*]."
3. An array of a doll, a skirt, a doll's shoe, a doll's bottle, a rattle, a spoon, a doll's blouse, and a toy. Tester says, "If I wanted to dress the doll, which things don't I need? Give them to me."
4. An array of a rubber ball, cookies, a pocketbook, grapes, a lollipop, a piece of clothing, a small book, and an egg. Tester says, "Give me the things that people can't eat."

---

[7]The term *exclusion* is intended to refer to concepts that are typified by terms such as *not, other than,* and *different from.* The constraints governing this type of demand can vary in a number of ways. In order to try to capture some of these variations, four types of items were developed. In particular, they focused on the generality of the item that had to be excluded, that is, whether it was a total category or a specific instance of a category, and the presence or absence of relevant objects. This first cluster is an example of a task in which the child must exclude a specific instance of a category while the relevant objects are in front of him or her.

L. Concepts: Citing an example by excluding a specific object
   total number in cluster: 4
1. sample item
Material none.
Task tester says, "Listen, a little girl wrote with something that was not a pencil. What thing could she have used?"
(See Appendix B, p. 147, for scoring.)
   Other items in this cluster are:
2. "A little boy drank something that was not milk. What could he have had to drink?"
3. "A little girl played with something that was not a doll. What could she have played with?"
4. "A man wore something that was not a coat. What could he have worn?"

M. Concepts: Citing an example by excluding a class of objects
   total number in cluster: 4
1. sample item
Material none.
Task tester says, "Listen, a lady was in the supermarket and saw something that was not food. What could she have seen?"
(See Appendix B, p. 147, for scoring.)
   Other items in this cluster are:
2. "The mother washed something that was not clothes. What could she have washed?"
3. "I walked down the street and saw something that had no wheels. What do you think I saw?"
4. "A little boy was at the zoo and saw something that was not an animal. What could he have seen?"

N. Concepts: Defining words
   total number in cluster: 4
1. sample item
Material none.
Task tester says, "Tell me what a cup is"[8]
(See Appendix B, p. 145, for scoring.)
   Other items in this cluster are:
2. "Tell me what a car is."
3. "Tell me what scissors are."

---

[8]These items followed items in I-F and II-F, in which instances of these objects had been seen by the child.

O. Unusual imitations
   total number in cluster: 7
1.   sample item
Material   none.
Task   tester says, "Now say this:*'What does the dog say?'* "[9]
(See Appendix B, p. 140, for scoring.)
   Other items in this cluster are:
2.   Tester says, "Now say this: *'Show me your pretty shoes.'* "
3.   Tester says, "Now say this: *'Your teacher is in the room.'*"
4.   Tester says, "I want you to do something, but before you do it, I want you to say what you're going to do. Listen—Walk to the door and open it."
5.   Two objects, a pencil and a box. The instructions are identical to those in number 4, but the command is, *"Put the pencil in the box."*
6.   Tester says, "I'm going to say something to you really loud and I want you to whisper it to me." Tester then says *(in loud voice)*, "The dog saw a bone."
7.   *Tester says,* "I'm going to whisper something to you and I want you to say it really loud to me." The tester then whispers, *"The dog saw a bone."*

GROUP IV: REASONING ABOUT PERCEPTION

The demands in this group are tapped by the following clusters of items:

A.   Predicting: Changes in position *(Where will . . .)*
B.   Predicting: Changes in structure *(What will happen if . . . ?)*
C.   Justifying a prediction *(Why will . . . ?)*
D.   Justifying a decision: Essential characteristics *(Why wouldn't it?)*
E.   Justifying a decision: Nonessential characteristics *(Why would it?)*
F.   Identifying the causes of an event *(What made it happen?)*
G.   Formulating a solution *(What could you do?)*
H.   Formulating a solution from another's perspective *(What could he [or she] do?)*
I.   Selecting the means to a goal *(What could we use?)*
J.   Explaining the means to a goal *(Why should we use that?)*
K.   Explaining the construction of objects *(Why is . . . made of that?)*
L.   Explaining an inference drawn from an observation *(How can we tell?)*

---

[9]Each of the sentences in this cluster came after the child had imitated two simple sentences from I-G. This procedure was adopted to help the child recognize that the task was one of imitation.

M. Explaining the logic of compound words *(Why is this called . . . ?)*
N. Explaining the obstacles to an action   *(Why can't we . . . ?)*

The specific items in each cluster are as follows.
A. Predicting: Changes in position
   total number in cluster: 2
1. Sample item
Material   consists of a doll and a small box. The doll is facing the child, and the box is behind the doll.
Task   tester says, "If I turn the doll so that she is facing the box, what part of her head will you see?"
(See Appendix B, p. 150, for scoring.)
   The other item in this cluster involves:
2. A doll placed in a seated position at the corner of a table. The tester says, "Look at the doll over here. Where would she be if she fell from the table?"
B. Predicting: Changes in structure
   total number in cluster: 5
1. sample item
Material   consists of a stack of four blocks, vertically arranged, going from bottom to top as follows: red, blue, yellow, and green.
Task   tester points to the block at the bottom and says, "What will happen to the pile of blocks if I take this one away?"
(See Appendix B, p. 153, for scoring.)
   Other items in this cluster are:
2. The four blocks are presented in a horizontal arrangement, with the red block at the end. Tester points to the red block and says, "What will happen to the pile of blocks if I take this one away?"
3. The child observes the working of a balance scale by the tester placing a clip on each side. The tester then holds up a clip, points to one end of the scale, and says, "What will happen if I put another clip in?"
4. Tester then points to the other end of the scale and says, "What will happen if I take a clip out?"
5. A clear, covered plastic vial is shown, filled three-quarters of the way with water. The tester presents the vial upside down, points to the cap, and says, "What will happen if I take this off?"

C. Justifying a prediction
   total number in cluster: 5
1. sample item
Material   consists of a stack of four blocks, vertically arranged, going from bottom to top as follows: red, blue, yellow, and green (the material is identical to the sample item in IV B).

Task   after the child has made his or her prediction to the question in the sample item in IV B, he or she is asked, "Why will that happen?" (See Appendix B, p. 153, for scoring.)

Other items in this cluster are:

2. After the child has made a prediction about the horizontally arranged blocks in the second item in IV-B, she or he is asked, "Why will that happen?"

3. Tester shows an empty bowl and a clear plastic bag containing marbles. Tester asks, "If this bowl were filled all the way up with play dough, could I pour the marbles inside?"[10] After the child responds, tester asks, "Why?" or "Why not?"

4. Tester shakes a box containing marbles and says, "Do you hear that noise?" After child responds, the tester says, "Yes, because there are marbles in the box. If there were no marbles in the box, would it still make a noise?" After child responds, tester asks, "Why?" or "Why not?"

5. Tester opens a book to a picture of some cats and asks, "What are these?" Tester then asks, "If the book were closed, would you still see the picture of the ——— [*using child's word*]?" After child responds, tester asks, "Why?" or "Why not?"

D. Justifying a decision: Essential characteristics
    total number in cluster: 2

1. sample item

Material   consists of two wooden semicircles and two wooden thin rectangular sticks.

Task   tester *(referring to the semicircles)* says, "I'm going to make a circle out of these," and proceeds to do so. Tester then separates the semicircles and places one next to each stick. Tester says, "If I had used these [*pointing to the sticks*] instead of these [*pointing to the semicircles*] to make the circle, would it still be a circle?" After child answers, tester asks, "Why?" or "Why not?"

(See Appendix B, p. 154, for scoring.)

The other item in this cluster involves:

2. A yellow, rectangular sponge; below it are a yellow paper triangle and a yellow sponge triangle. The tester says, "If the sponge were made of this [*pointing to the paper triangle*] and not this [*pointing to the*

---

[10]This item and the next two in this cluster and all items in IV-D and IV-E demand a yes–no response. However, the yes–no part is not scored since by chance there is a 50 percent probability of its being correct. These questions have to be asked, however, if the "why" question (i.e., the request for justification that follows) is to be meaningful.

sponge triangle], would it still be a sponge?" After child responds, tester asks, "Why?" or "Why not?"

E. Justifying a decision: Nonessential characteristics
   total number in cluster: 2
1. sample item
Material   consists of two red wooden semicircles in the form of a circle, one red paper rectangle, and one blue paper rectangle.
Task   tester says, "If the circle were made of this color [*pointing to the blue*] instead of this color [*pointing to the red*], would it still be a circle?" After child responds, tester asks, "Why?" or "Why not?"
(See Appendix B, p. 154, for scoring.)
   The other item in this cluster involves:
2. a blue, rectangular sponge. Below it are a blue paper circle and a blue paper rectangle. Tester says, "If this sponge were this shape [*pointing to the blue circle*] instead of this shape [*pointing to the blue rectangle*], would it still be a sponge?" After child responds, tester asks, "Why?" or "Why not?"

F. Identifying the causes of an event
   total number in cluster: 2
1. sample item
Material   consists of a flashlight with the light on.
Task   tester says, "Turn the light off." Tester then says, "How did the light go off?"
(See Appendix B, p. 156, for scoring.)
   The other item in this cluster involves:
2. A ball and the lid of a box. The tester pushes the ball so that it rolls from one end of the lid to the other. The tester then says, "What made the ball move?"

G. Formulating a solution
   total number in cluster: 2
1. sample item
Material   consists of 15 small items spread out on table; array includes a lollipop, a toy gun, a paper shopping bag, a sponge, and two balls.
Task   tester points to material and says, "If I wanted you to carry all these things over to that table, tell me what you could use so that you could carry them all at the same time."
(See Appendix B, p. 156, for scoring.)
   The other item in this cluster involves:
2. A small box with 15 small items (e.g., a box of crayons, play money, a doll's shoe, a sock); a large box is also present. Tester tries (unsuccessfully) to fit the items into the small box and says, "These things

just keep falling out of the box. What could we use so that the things would fit and not keep falling out?''

H. Formulating a solution from another's perspective
   total number in cluster: 1
1. sample item
Material   consists of a picture of a boy facing a girl in a room. There is a sink in the background which is in the girl's line of sight but is not visible to the boy.
Task   tester says, ''The boy wants to get a drink but he cannot see the sink. What should the girl tell him so that he can find the sink?''
(See Appendix B, p. 148, for scoring.)
Note: This task combines the role-taking skills of III-C with the problem-solving skills of IV G and I.

I. Selecting the means to a goal
   total number in cluster: 4
1. sample item
Material   consists of three stars (each with five points); one star with one of the five points removed; an array that contains tape, scissors, chalk, the outline of a star, two semicircles, and three triangles (each equal to one of the points of the stars).
Task   tester points to the three intact stars and says, ''I want to change these stars so that they look like this one [*pointing to the star with the point cut off*]. Which one of these things should I use? [*pointing to the array*]''
(See Appendix B, p. 162, for scoring.)
   Other items in this cluster involve:
2. Tester shows a single star and says *(pointing),* ''These are the sharp points of the star. I don't want the sharp points on it any more.'' Tester shows the same array as in sample item and asks, ''Which one of these things should I use so that there won't be any sharp points on the star?''
3. Tester pours beads through a funnel into a glass jar and then says, ''I don't want the beads to go through this thing any more'' [*pointing to the hole in the funnel*]. An array is shown containing a button, a tooth-pick, a cork, a paper clip, a piece of netting, and a safety pin. Tester asks, ''Which one of these things should I use to stop the beads from going through?''
4. Tester presents a paper cup with the bottom cut out. The cup is shown to the child and the tester says, ''Water won't stay in this cup.'' An array is shown that consists of six different pieces of paper—a circular piece adequate to fit the bottom, a circular piece that is too small, a circular piece of adequate size but which contains holes, a square piece of

paper, a circular piece made of thin tissue paper, and a circular piece with a donut-shaped hole in the center. Tester asks, "Which one of these should I use to fix the cup so that the water stays in?"

J. Explaining the means to a goal
   total number in cluster: 4
1. Sample item
Material consists of the array from the sample item in IV I.
Task after the child has selected an item from the array (in the sample item in IV-I), tester asks, "Why did you pick that one?"
(See Appendix B, p. 157, for scoring.)
   Other items in this cluster involve:
2. Tester asks, *why did you pick that one,* after child has made his or her choice in IV-I (2).
3. Tester asks, *why did you pick that one,* after child has made his or her choice in IV-I (3).
4. Tester asks, *why did you pick that one,* after child has made his or her choice in IV-I (4).
Note: These items bear a similarity to those in IV-G. These items differ, however, in that they are based on a subtle multiple-choice situation (whereas the IV'G items involve no such potentially confusing choices) and that they require the children to rationalize their choices. Hence, the items are placed in different clusters. In all these items, however, the children are given a specified goal (e.g., changing the stars to look like the model shown). They must then determine a course of action that is appropriate to meeting that goal (e.g., cutting) and the instrument or means necessary for carrying out the course of action (e.g., scissors).

K. Explaining the construction of objects
   total number in cluster: 3
1. sample item
Material consists of a key, a board with a piece of gold metal, and a piece of gold cloth.
Task tester shows the key saying, "This is a key to open a door." Tester then displays the board and says, "Keys are made of metal like this [*pointing to metal*] and not material like this [*pointing to material*]. Why do you think keys are made of this and not this?"
(See Appendix B, p. 158, for scoring.)
   Other items in this cluster involve:
2. A mirror and a board with a piece of shiny metal and a piece of thick cardboard. Tester shows the mirror saying, "This is a mirror that we look in." Tester then displays the board and says, "Mirrors are made of shiny material like this [*pointing*] and not cardboard like this [*point-

ing]. Why do you think mirrors are made of things like this and not things like this?"

3. A red rubber boot and a board with a piece of red rubber and a piece of red tissue paper. Tester points to boot and says, "This is what children wear on rainy and snowy days." Tester then displays the board and says, "Boots are made of rubber like this [*pointing*] and not of paper like this [*pointing*]. Why do you think that boots are made of rubber like this and not paper like this?"

L. Explaining an inference drawn from an observation
    total number in cluster: 2
1. sample item
Material   consists of two pictures—one is of a smiling girl standing; the other is of a girl not smiling, seated on the limb of a tree.
Task   tester says, "This girl is happy [*pointing to the smiling girl*] and this one is not happy [*pointing to the other picture*]. How do I know which one is happy?"
(See Appendix B, p. 158, for scoring.)
   The other item in this cluster involves:
2. Two pictures of the same car; one has all the wheels in place, and the other has one of the wheels lying by the side of the car. Tester says *(pointing)*, "This car is good and this one is not good. How can you tell it's not good?"

M. Explaining the logic of compound words
    total number in cluster: 3
1. sample item
Material   consists of a board with a piece of fabric (that contains a buttonhole) and a lock (that contains a keyhole).
Task   tester says *(pointing)*, "This is a buttonhole and this is a keyhole. Why do we call this [*pointing*] a 'buttonhole' and not a 'buttonmaker?' "
(See Appendix B, p. 157, for scoring.)
   Other items in this cluster involve:
2. A paper towel and a turkish towel. Tester says *(pointing)*, "This is a paper towel and this is a regular towel. Why do we call this [*pointing*] a 'paper' towel and not a 'turkish' towel?"
3. A doll's plastic raincoat and a doll's winter coat are shown. Tester says *(pointing)*, "This is a raincoat and this is a winter coat. Why do we call this [*pointing*] a 'raincoat' and not a 'sporty' coat?"

N. Explaining the obstacles to an action
    total number in cluster: 6
1. sample item
Material   consists of a fully completed puzzle of a bird; in addition, there is a duplicate of one of the pieces of the puzzle (the bird's face).

Task tester says, "This is a puzzle." The tester holds up the duplicate (extra) piece and asks, "Why can't we fit this piece in the puzzle?" (See Appendix B, p. 158, for scoring.)

Other items in this cluster are:

2. A closed, clear plastic box is shown that contains small, white buttons. Tester says, "Look at the buttons. Why can't we touch them?"

3. A closed book with a red-checked cover is shown. Tester says, "There are pictures in this book. Why can't we see the pictures now?"

4. A deck of cards is present; the picture on one of the cards is shown to the child. The card is then put back into the deck, face down. Tester says, "Why can't we see that picture anymore?"

5. An open plastic box that contains rods of different sizes and colors is present. Tester produces (not from the box) a small, red rod and says, "Look at this. Now watch." The tester then places the rod in the box and mixes it in with all the other rods. (Several of the rods in the box are identical to the rod that was mixed in.) Tester says, "Why is it very hard to find the one that I was just holding?"

6. Two yellow, wooden blocks are shown. A blue rod is nailed on one of the blocks; the other block holds an identical, but unattached rod. Tester moves the unattached rod across the board and says, "Look, I can move this one." Tester then tries to move the nailed rod and asks, "Why can't I move this rod across the board?"

Appendix B

Scoring the Responses

This appendix continues the detailing of the test. Appendix A offered a description of the items that are presented to the children, while Appendix B contains the scoring used in evaluating the responses that the children give to these items. The presentation here parallels that used in Appendix A in that detailed examples are shown only for the sample items. The remaining items in each cluster are evaluated in ways similar to the sample item. Because of limitations of space, however, the actual scoring is not shown. In an effort to aid the reader's integration of the two appendixes, all items in Appendix B are labeled (both by title and group number) as they appear in Appendix A.

Two basic patterns of scoring are used in evaluating the children's responses. The rules that govern these patterns are outlined on pages 138 and 160. For both patterns, the responses are coded from Fully Adequate responses to responses of increasingly lower degrees of adequacy. Each of the various levels of adequacy is assigned a weighted score; 3 points for Fully Adequate, 2 points for Acceptable, 1 point for Ambiguous, and 0 points for Inadequate. These point values are shown in their appropriate places on each page of the scoring (e.g., the number 3 is in the box with Fully Adequate, the number 2 is in the box with Acceptable, and so forth). Immediately following the explanation of each pattern of scoring are all the items that are evaluated according to that pattern. In all cases, representative samples of the children's responses are given to illustrate the coding used. All categories of responses are illustrated except those from the I Don't Know and No Response categories. No examples are offered from these two categories since the behaviors representing these categories do not vary from one item to the next. In occasional instances a category does not apply to certain items (e.g., an ambiguous response is not possible). In these cases, "not applicable" is written in the appropriate place on the scoring sheet. Given the complexity and variety of language possible in answering the questions, it is clear that a wide variety of responses can be, and have been, obtained. We recognize that our coding for any particular response can well be questioned by the reader. We hope, however, that undue attention is not directed to the validity of the coding for any single response. Instead, our aim here is to develop a reasonable and reliable method for coding that would be applicable to the vast array of responses that children give to the demands of the test that we have developed.

Table B-1   The following pattern of scoring was used on all items in which the child had to produce a verbal response to a problem. In general the following criteria guided the scoring.

Score of 3 Fully Adequate	Child offers a valid response that fully meets the demands of the problem posed (childish grammar is not penalized).
Score of 2 Acceptable but: a. Imprecise	Child gives a valid response but only implicitly refers to the relevant information or formulates it in a way that renders the response less precise and focused.
b. Oblique	The response, while technically correct, does not focus on the central issue.
c. Adds extraneous information	The response is adequate but includes additional irrelevant or invalid information that weakens or detracts from the answer.
Score of 1 Ambiguous	The response is formulated in such a way that it is unclear whether it is adequate or not. [The examples in this category are followed by scores that indicate where the ambiguity rests; for example 2a/0b indicates that the response could either be Acceptable–Imprecise (2a) or Inadequate–Association to Material (0b).]
Score of 0 Inadequate: a. Invalid Formulation	The response shows some grasp of the question but the answer is incorrect.
b. Association to material	The child's response shows little or no understanding of the question, but it is focused on the material (either it is a description of the material or a response strongly associated to the material).
c. Irrelevant Verbalization	The response shows no understanding of the question or the material. Often it is marked by references to people (including the child), references to action (e.g., telling tester to act on the material), or an imitation of all or part of the adult's words or actions.
d. I Don't Know*	Child states that she or he cannot answer the problem.
e. No Response*	Child offers no response to the problem or just shrugs.

*These two categories are not repeated on the sample items that follow since the behaviors representing these categories do not vary from one item to the next.

Table B-2 *Naming an object*

	Heard (Cluster I-D)	Touched (Cluster I-E)	Seen (Cluster I-F)
	(What did you hear?)	*(What did you touch?)*	*(What is this?)*
Fully Adequate 3	*Bell.* Correctly labels object selected (e.g., whistle, harmonica, rattle).	*Ball.* Correctly labels object selected (e.g., yo-yo, styrofoam disc, wax pear).	*Cup.* *Yellow cup.* *Toy cup.*
Acceptable but: Imprecise 2a	*A ringing thing.*	*You bounce and throw it.*	*For drinking.*
Oblique 2b			
Adds Extraneous 2c	Says *bell* or names object selected and names one additional item in array.	Says *ball* or object selected and names one additional item in array.	*A coffee cup.* *Tea cup.* *A drinking cup.*
Ambiguous 1	Says *bell* after having selected another object (in identifying an object by sound) (3/0b).	Says *ball* after having selected another object (in identifying an object by touch) (3/0b).	*Drink* (2a/Ob).
Inadequate: Invalid 0a	Labels any item in array other than his or her selection.	Labels any item in array other than his or her selection.	*Glass.*
Association 0b	Labels an item not in the array.	Labels an item not in the array.	*You use it.* *A coffee.*
Irrelevant 0c			*I have that at home.*

Table B-3   Sentence imitation or completion

	Imitating a Simple Sentence (cluster I-g)	Completing a Sentence (cluster II-E)	Unusual Imitations (Cluster III-O)
	(Say this.)	*(Finish this.)*	*(Say this.)*
Fully Adequate 3	*The ball was in the house.*	*Food.* *Dinner.* *I like to eat some candy.*	*What does the dog say?*
Acceptable but: Imprecise 2a	*A ball was in the house.* *Ball was in the house.*		*What does a dog say?* *What did the dog say?*
Oblique 2b	*Now say this. The ball was in the house.*		*Now say this. What does the dog say?*
Adds Extraneous 2c	*The ball was in the house and he played with it.*		*What does the dog say? Ruff ruff.*
Ambiguous 1		*Meal (2a/Ob).* *Dog food (2c/Ob).*	
Inadequate: Invalid 0a	*A ball rolled in the street.*	*Water.* *Soda.*	*The dog say.*
Association 0b	*'Cause it was raining.*	*Fork.* *Dishes.*	*Ruff ruff.* *Bow wow.*
Irrelevant 0c	*I can play ball.*	*Horses.* *I'm hungry.*	*In his house.*

Table B-4   Remembering

	Pictured Objects (cluster I-H)	Incidental Information (Cluster I-I)
	(What did you see?)	(What did you see?)
Fully Adequate 3	Offers any three or more of the following five labels or their synonyms: kettle, toaster, flower, carriage, coat.	Offers any three or more of the following five labels or their synonyms: spoon, book, ball, apple, pencil.
Acceptable but: Imprecise 2a	Offers any two of the above labels.	Offers any two of the above labels.
Oblique 2b	——————————————Not	Applicable ———————————→
Adds Extraneous 2c	Offers any two or more of the above labels plus labels for items not in the array (e.g., pencil).	Offers any two or more of the above labels plus labels for items not in the array (e.g., dress).
Ambiguous 1	——————————————Not	Applicable ———————————→
Inadequate: Invalid 0a	Offers any one of the above labels; in addition may label items not in the array.	Offers any one of the above labels; in addition may label items not in the array.
Association 0b	Offers only labels for items not in the array.	Offers only labels for items not in the array.
Irrelevant 0c		

Table B-5   Describing

	A Scene (cluster II-B)	Events Subsequent to a Scene (cluster III-B)
	(What is happening?)	*(What will happen next?)*
Fully Adequate 3	*They're eating.* *The baby's gonna have coffee.* *The sister is the mother, and they're making believe they're playing house.*	*Put the stuff away.* *She might play outside.* *Go to bed.*
Acceptable but: Imprecise 2a	*They're playing.* *They're pouring coffee.* *Mommy poured tea in there.*	*Put them away.*
Oblique 2b	*The chair is breaking* [referring to a break in the line drawing of the chair]. *Water is spilling* [referring to the coffee being poured].	*She might forget to clean up.* *Get up.* *She's going to pick up all these* [points to cup].
Adds Extraneous 2c	*The mother is pouring the drink into a cup and she doesn't have any hands.*	
Ambiguous 1	*Eating* (2a/0b).	*Play* (2a/0b). *She plays* (2a/0b).
Inadequate: Invalid 0a	*She can't reach the apple.* *She broke her chair.* *She's leaving the table.*	*She might come back.* *The baby would cry.*
Association 0b	*The coffee, the baby.* *This one had been broken, and this one has a different color.*	*She giving her some coffee.* *Eat.*
Irrelevant 0c	*There's no chair.*	*Broke the table.*

Table B-6   *Recalling*

	Items Named in a Statement (cluster II-C)	Information from a Statement (cluster II-D)		
				Purpose
		Subject	Location	What?)
	(What things....?)	(Who?)	(Where?)	
Fully Adequate 3	Says, cat and lady.	James and Ann. Jamie and Ann.	Down the street. On the sidewalk. To their friends.	Their friends' new car. A car.
Acceptable but: Imprecise 2a	Says either cat or lady.	James. Ann. Jamie.	Street. Lane. Road.	Car.
Oblique 2b			To the car. Outside.	New thing.
Adds Extraneous 2c	Says either cat or both cat and lady and then adds other labels.	Jane and Ann. Janet Ann. Jane and James.	Down the street and they found their friend the car. They were walking to see that on the sidewalk.	Car and a train. Down the stairs and a new car. Their friends' Daddy's car.
Ambiguous 1				Toy (2a/0b).
Inadequate: Invalid 0a		A boy and a girl. Offers one or two incorrect names (e.g., Bobby and Mary).		Their friends' bus. Their friends.

continued

143

Table B-6   *Recalling* continued

| | Items Named in a Statement (cluster II-C) | Information from a Statement (cluster II-D) | | |
| | | Subject | Location | Purpose |
	(What things....?)	(Who?)	(Where?)	(What?)
Association 0b	Only offers labels other than cat or lady.	New car.	Home. To the park. To the house.	The brothers. A dog. The puppet show.
Irrelevant 0c		My teacher. My friends.	They went by car.	It's a song.

Table B-7 Concepts and definitions

	Concepts: Naming Characteristics and Functions of Objects (cluster II-F)			Defining Words (cluster III-N)
	Function *(Tell me its . . . .)*	Part-Whole Relationship *(Tell me its . . . .)*	Physical Attribute *(Tell me its . . . .)*	*(What is a . . . ?)*
Fully Adequate 3	*Drink from it.* *Drink out of it.* *Drink.*	*We hold it.* *We hold the handle.*	*Yellow.*	*A thing you drink from.* *Something you drink out of.* *Something that's round, has a handle, and you pour stuff in it.*
Acceptable but: Imprecise 2a	*Drink it.*	*Pick it up.* *Hold.* *Hold it on with your hand.*		*It's round and it's colored.* *For drink.* *A round thing.*
Oblique 2b	*Hold it.* *Put liquids in it.* *Play with it.*	*We put our hands in.* *We put our fingers on it.* *Put your finger through.*	*Like this paper* [points to yellow paper].	
Adds Extraneous 2c	*We drink some coffee.* *Put milk in it and drink it.*	*Take it with your hand and drink the coffee.* *We take it and we drink it.*		*A cup is a glass you drink from it.* *You drink out of and you wash.* *A cup is a coffee cup that people drink out of.*
Ambiguous 1	*Use it* (2b/0b). *Wash it* (2b/0b).	*We drink like this* [gestures] (2a/0b).		*Hold and then you drink* (2a/0b). *That's why you drink it* (2a/0b). *A cup is something to drink* (2a/0b).

continued

Table B-7   Concepts and definitions continued

	Concepts: Naming Characteristics and Functions of Objects			Defining Words (cluster III-N)
	Function (Tell me its . . . .)	Part-Whole Relationship (cluster II-F) (Tell me its . . . .)	Physical Attribute (Tell me its . . . .)	(What is a . . . ?)
Inadequate: Invalid 0a	Eat with it.	It hold the finger. That's for holding on your finger.	Pink. White.	Child gestures drinking but offers no verbalization. Made out of paper.
Association 0b	Tea or coffee. Coffee.	You take some water. A handle. The cup.	Round. Plastic.	A glass. Soda.
Irrelevant 0c	Put it in the bank.	Put it right here [points to floor]. Mommy have one.		

146

Table B-8 *Differences and similarities*

	Identifying Differences (cluster II-H) *(How are these different?)*	Identifying Similarities (Cluster III-I) *(How are these the same?)*
Fully Adequate 3	*This is a scissors and this is a knife. This one cuts chicken or meat and this one cuts paper or cardboard.*	*Because they both cut.* *They the same because this one to cut something and this one to cut something.* *They can both cut but one can't cut paper and one can cut paper.*
Acceptable but: Imprecise 2a	*One is long and one is short.* *These have two holes [scissors] and this doesn't [knife].*	*Both could hurt you.* *This has a point and this has a point.*
Oblique 2b	*'Cause you hold this [knife] with your hand and this [scissors] with your fingers.*	*People could use both of them.*
Adds Extraneous 2c	*That's a scissors and this like the scissors, but it's a knife.* *'Cause this has blades [points to serrated edge of knife], and it's a knife, and this is a scissors.*	*They both can hurt you and they both sharp, and this is a knife and this is a scissor.* *They not the same—they both cut.*
Ambiguous 1	*This is a scissors (2a/0b).* *This is a different shape and this is a different shape (2a/0b).*	*This one's to cut meat, this one's to cut paper (2c/0b).* *'Cause this is a scissor and its cuts, this is a knife and it cuts (2c/0b).*

continued

147

Table B-8   *Differences and similarities* continued

	Identifying Differences (cluster II-H)	Identifying Similarities (Cluster III-I)
	(How are these different?)	*(How are these the same?)*
Inadequate: Invalid 0a	*This belongs in a drawer* [points to knife] *and this belongs on a table* [points to scissors]. *One is used for cutting things that are hard.*	*They both cut meat.*
Association 0b	*Both cut.* *This cuts and this cuts.* *Not the same.*	*One is a scissor, and one is a knife.* *This has a sharp point, but this cuts.* *This is a scissor, this is not, this is too small.*
Irrelevant 0c	*Right there* [points to booklet].	*Not that one.* *What are these?*

148

Table B-9   Concepts: Citing an example

	Within a Category (cluster II-I)	By Excluding a Specific Object (cluster III-L)	By Excluding a Class of Objects (cluster III-M)
	(Name something that is a . . . .)	(Name something that can . . . . but is not a . . . .)	(Name something that is not a . . . .)
Fully Adequate 3	Car. Bike. Wagon.	Crayon. Magic marker. Chalk.	A cash register. Shopping basket. Sponge.
Acceptable but: Imprecise 2a	The wheels of a car.		
Oblique 2b		Finger.	A dog.
Adds Extraneous 2c	Wheels? On the car in front or back?	A crayon or a stick. Crayon on a coloring book.	Toys for the witch to eat. Some potato chips and toy rifles.
Ambiguous 1		Stick (2b/0a). Feather (3/0c).	Lollipop (2b/0b). Soda (2b/0b). Car (2b/0b).
Inadequate: Invalid 0a	A car with no wheels.	A pencil but it didn't have black on it.	Person.
Association 0b	It rolls. Some tires.	Paper. A color. A sharpen.	Dog food. Fruit.
Irrelevant 0c	My daddy has a wheel. Pencil. Wind got wheel broken.	Monster and a boogie man. A rock.	Wicked witch. She got lunch. She could see breakfast.

Table B-10   *Formulating statements*

	Assuming the Role of Another Person (cluster III-C)	Formulating a Set of Directions (cluster III-F)	Formulating a Solution from Another's Perspective (cluster IV-H)
	(What could . . . say?)	*(Tell me how . . . .)*	*(What could he do?)*
Fully Adequate 3	*They would say: Where's the other shoe?* *You look funny.* *How come you have only one shoe on?*	*Put on the same thing that is the same and cover it and say: What did you see?* *You would have to put the pictures on the right thing.*	*Come over here and come straight in there and stop when you see the sink.* *Tell him to go in there, to turn around and walk in the bathroom.*
Acceptable but: Imprecise 2a	*You go with one shoe on.*	*I say to her: You put a shoe there, a baby there, a cat there, a block there.* *You play the game and then you do like this [gestures matching].*	*You go this way and that and then you see it [points from boy to sink].*
Oblique 2b	*Come here, teacher.* *They didn't say nothing—they laughed.*	*Look carefully.* *Please play.*	*She should tell him where to go.* *Go in the kitchen and find the sink.*
Adds Extraneous 2c	*They said to their teacher: The little girl had her shoe off.* *He said: Where is your shoe at?*		*Move over closer.*

Ambiguous 1	*The boy is wearing one shoe (3/0d).* *He gotta go get another shoe (3/0b).* *Put his other shoe on (2a/0a).*	*Play the game (2b/0d).* *To match the pictures (2a/0b).* *I say I play with you two times (2c/0a).*	*It's in the bathroom (2a/0b).* *To turn around (2a/0a).* *Go that way (2a/0b).*
Inadequate: Invalid 0a	*They laughed at him.* *Who brought that to school?* *Where my shoes go?*		*He should tell her that it's in the bathroom.* *She should push him where the sink is.*
Association 0b	*They have two shoes on.* *The boy put the other shoe on.*	*You told me to put the pictures on the board.* *I say yes.*	*Child makes path with fingers to the sink but says nothing.* *Child points to sink and says: Sink.* *The boy has to turn around.*
Irrelevant 0c	*No more one shoe, two shoes.* *You take your shoes and go to bed.*	*I got two brothers.* *I'm going to take it home.*	*I'd ask my mommy for water.*

Table B-11 *Following sequenced directions and predicting changes*

	Following a Set of Directions (cluster III-D)	Predicting: Change in Position (cluster IV-A)
	(Do this . . . then this . . . .)	*(Where will . . . ?)*
Fully Adequate 3	Performs the following three actions in the correct order: takes socks off doll, puts hat in box, puts box on floor.	*The back of her hair.* Child points to back of head. *Hair* [points to back of head].
Acceptable but: Imprecise 2a	Performs two of the above three actions in the correct order.	*Back.* *Nothing, in the back, no face.*
Oblique 2b	Performs all three actions but in the wrong order.	*The other side.*
Adds Extraneous 2c	Performs all three actions plus actions not requested (e.g., takes the dress off the doll).	
Ambiguous 1		*Neck* (2a/0b). *Hair* [without pointing] (2a/0b).
Inadequate: Invalid 0a	Performs two of the three actions in any order as well as actions not requested.	*Hair* [points incorrectly]. *She would see the door.* *The top.*
Association 0b	Performs one of the three actions with or without actions not requested.	*Legs.* *You can see her face.*
Irrelevant 0c	Performs only actions not requested.	*The box.* *Dolls can move.* *A birthday.*

Table B-12 *Formulating*

	A Generalization about a Set of Events (cluster III-G)	A Statement to Unify a Sequence of Pictures (cluster III-H)
	(What happened to all of these?)	*(Tell this story.)*
Fully Adequate 3	*It became colors.* *They turned into all the colors.* *They got different colors.*	*It's getting filled up.* *It got filled with water.* *There once was a faucet that was leaking and it dripped into a cup and it got full, full, fullest.*
Acceptable but: Imprecise 2a	*It's changed.* *It turned red, green, blue, and yellow.* *It made them a different color.*	*Here the water is about to go in the glass and it's half full and here is more full and here it's a lot of full.* *First it was empty, then it got a little bit more, and then it got bigger one.*
Oblique 2b	*It became swirls.*	
Adds Extraneous 2c	*They colored and we can't drink it.*	
Ambiguous 1	*Colors* (2a/0b). *It's gone* (2a/0a).	*Empty, full, full, and full* [pointing to each picture] (2a/0b).

continued

Table B-12 Formulating continued

	A Generalization about a Set of Events (cluster III-G)	A Statement to Unify a Sequence of Pictures (cluster III-H)
	(What happened to all of these?)	(Tell this story.)
Inadequate: Invalid 0a	It got wet. Nothing. It melted.	This one got water; this one has more [treating each picture as a different glass]. The glass don't get none in but these did.
Association 0b	This red, red, green, blue, and yellow. You mixed them. The water is down in the stuff.	The glass is not filled with water. The water came down a glass [pointing to one picture]. It's dripping.
Irrelevant 0c	Because you got to.	The glass broke. When the water come in the glass, it spills on your head like that. You dropped it.

Table B-13   Concepts

	Selecting an Object by Exclusion (cluster III-J)	Selecting a Set of Objects by Exclusion (cluster III-K)
	(What else . . . ?)	*(Find the things that are not . . .)*
Fully Adequate 3	Selects pen.	Leaves the dolls and selects all of the following objects: ball, rattle, rubber animal.
Acceptable but: Imprecise 2a		Leaves the dolls and selects two of the above objects.
Oblique 2b		
Adds Extraneous 2c	Initially selects the pen and then offers one additional object.	Initially selects two or more of the above objects and then offers one doll.
Ambiguous 1	Selects ink or paintbrush (2b/0a).	
Inadequate: Invalid	Selects one object other than the pen and then selects the pen.	Initially selects the above object and then offers the dolls.
Association 0b	Selects one or more objects other than the pen.	Selects only a doll or dolls.
Irrelevant 0c	Selects all the objects	Offers all the objects

155

Table B-14   Predictions

	Predicting: Change in Structure (cluster IV-B)	Justifying a Prediction (cluster IV-C)
	(What will happen if . . . ?)	*(Why will . . . ?)*
Fully Adequate 3	*It would fall down.* *It might fall.* *It will fall.*	[*it will fall*]* *Because it won't have anything to hold it up.* [*it will fall*]* *Because that's on the bottom.* [*it will fall*]* *If you take this one out* [*points to red*] *it won't be there to hold them up.*
Acceptable but: Imprecise 2a	*Fall.* *Another will fall off.*	[*it will fall*]* *Because it's placed on.* [*the yellow would be in the middle*]* *Because you wouldn't have that one* [*points to red*] *there.*
Oblique 2b	*The blue one* [next in stack] *will go down on the table.* *There will be three.* *It will get lower.*	[*there will be three*]* *Because you took a block away.*
Ambiguous 1	*Three* (2b/0b).	
Inadequate: Invalid 0a	*There will be more.* *It will turn into* [holds up five fingers].	[*it will fall*]* *Because it can't stand up* [points to red] *with another one off of it.*
Association 0b	*That's red.*	[*it will fall*]* [child demonstrates tumbling while saying]. *See, if you took this one away.* [*it will fall*]* *Cause if you take this out* [points to red] *it will fall.*
Irrelevant 0c	*We gonna hide it.* *We could.*	*I can build a house.*

*Child's response to Predicting: Change in Structure IV-B.

Table B-15 *Justifying a decision*

	Essential Characteristics (cluster IV-D) *(Why wouldn't it?)*	Nonessential Characteristics (cluster IV-E) *(Why would it?)*
Fully Adequate 3	'Cause these two things |points to sticks| ain't round. 'Cause it wouldn't still be the shape of a circle. 'Cause a circle doesn't have lines.	Because if that was blue and that was still round it would still be a circle. 'Cause it would just be a different color. 'Cause if you made it out of any color it would still be a circle 'cause it's still round.
Acceptable but: Imprecise 2a	Because lines like that will make a t and these |points to arcs| will make an o. 'Cause it would be like a square.	'Cause some blocks is white and brown and all different colors. 'Cause a circle could be red or blue or pink or orange or yellow.
Oblique 2b	They're too hard—if they were cardboard they could bend to a circle.	
Adds Extraneous 2c	Because these are straight lines and it has to be like a very short c.	'Cause this red and this red and it would be a circle if it's painted blue.
Ambiguous 1	'Cause circles are round and squares are flat (2c/0a). 'Cause these are sticks (2a/0b). 'Cause this goes like this |makes L with sticks| and this goes like this |makes circle with arcs| (2a/0b).	'Cause it will be like this |points to circle| (2a/0b). 'Cause it's round (2a/0b).

continued

Table B-15 *Justifying a decision* continued

	Essential Characteristics (cluster IV-D) *(Why wouldn't it?)*	Nonessential Characteristics (cluster IV-E) *(Why would it?)*
Inadequate: Invalid 0a	*'Cause it be another circle.* *'Cause it's not together.*	*'Cause the circle don't have to be blue; it have to be red.* *Because it would be a square.* *'Cause circles are only red.*
Association 0b	*'Cause they are this* [points to arcs]. *'Cause they the same.*	*'Cause this red and this red and this blue.* *'Cause that's a square and that's a circle.* *'Cause this one is black and this one is red.*
Irrelevant 0c	*'Cause it's all covered.* *'Cause I'll shown you* [plays with materials].	*When the record player goes it's a circle.* *I made it.* *Plays with materials.*

Table B-16   Means—ends formulations

	Identifying the Causes of an Event (cluster IV-F) *(What made it happen?)*	Formulating a Solution (cluster IV-G) *(What could you do?)*
Fully Adequate 3	*I did—I turned it off.* *I pushed this* [points to switch]. *With the switch.*	*Put all the stuff in the bag and then carry it.* *A bag.* Child selects shopping bag.
Acceptable but: Imprecise 2a	Child demonstrates action, with no verbalization. Child points to switch with no verbalization or says: *This.*	
Oblique 2b		*You could help me.*
Adds Extraneous 2c	*'Cause I push it off and you turn it off.*	
Ambiguous 1	*Down* (2a/0b). *Because I did that* (2a/0a).	*Carry this bag* (2a/0c). *Bag* (2a/0b).
Inadequate: Invalid 0a	*I pushed it up and down.*	*Maybe you could carry one at a time.* *My hands.*
Association 0b	*I put it back on.*	*Gun* [labeling object on table]. Child picks up one or more items and attempts to carry them.
Irrelevant 0c		Plays with items. *You could bounce the ball.*

Table B-17   Explaining

	The Means to a Goal (cluster IV-J)	The Logic of Compound Words (cluster IV-M)
	(Why should we use that?)	*(Why is this called . . . ?)*
Fully Adequate 3	(Selected scissors.)* *Because it could cut.* (Selected scissors.)* *You can cut it off like that.* (Selected scissors.)* *Because the scissor you can cut things with.*	*Because it's a hole.* *Because it's used to put buttons in.* *'Cause if it was a buttonmaker it wouldn't be on there, it would be a small person.*
Acceptable but: Imprecise 2a	*You got to cut it to make it like the other one.* *'Cause you could change them with that.*	
Oblique 2b	(Selected scissors.)* *'Cause is for you could cut and these is not for you to cut.*	
Adds Extraneous 2c	(Selected scissors.)* *The one cut the star and it look ahead.*	*'Cause this has a button to go in but it's not on top of this.*
Ambiguous 1	*'Cause it's a scissor* (2a/0b).	*That's why you put a button in here, that's for a shirt* (2c/0b). *Because it has that little thing that you put in the buttons* (2a/0b).

Inadequate: Invalid 0a		Because there's no button. 'Cause buttonholes can fit in the buttons.
Association 0b	(Selected outline.)* It would make a star. (Selected loose points.)* You use it on there. (Selected loose points.)* 'Cause that all got points.	Because that belongs to a coat. A keyhole—you gotta open the door. Because the button is on this side and the hole is on this side.
Irrelevant 0c	(Selected tape.)* Because you put tape there and all people fall down.	Where are the keys? You pull this up. 'Cause everybody lose the button to it.

*Response to Selecting Means to a Goal IV-I.

Table B-18   *Explaining*

	The Construction of Objects (cluster IV-K)	An Inference Drawn from an Observation (cluster IV-L)	The Obstacles to an Action (cluster IV-N)
	(Why is . . . made of that?)	*(How can we tell?)*	*(Why can't we . . . ?)*
Fully Adequate 3	*So they won't bend when they fit in the keyhole.* *A key is supposed to be hard, not material.*	*This one is happy because she got a big smile.* *'Cause you could see that expression on her face.*	*Because you have another one* |points to same piece in puzzle|. *There's already one here.*
Acceptable but: Imprecise 2a	*If this were hard, it would work.*	*She looks happy because of her face.* *'Cause it's laughing.*	*Because there's no space.* *Someone already made the puzzle.*
Oblique 2b			*If you took one out, you could put that one in.*
Adds Extraneous 2c	*Because keys are supposed to be hard in case you drop them they won't break.* *'Cause this rips sometimes.*	*Because her standing up and smiling.*	*Because this is in* |points to same piece in puzzle| *and it's sticking.* *'Cause there's not a shape for that.*
Ambiguous 1	*This is soft and this is hard (2a/0b).* *'Cause you can't use that* |points to material| *(2a/0b).*	*'Cause they're different (2a/0b).* *Cause this one has its mouth open and this one doesn't (2c/0b).*	*The bird is already there (2a/0a).* *You don't need it (2a/0c).* *Because it doesn't belong (2a/0b).*

Inadequate: Invalid 0a		'Cause she's looking down like she's happy.	Because it's too big. The bird is big and this is big and it don't fit.
Association 0b	Keys are for doors. 'Cause you sew it. 'Cause this is cloth, this is iron or steel.	They have different clothes. Because this one got shoes on. She doesn't have another foot.	Tries to fit piece in without making any verbal response. The bird is walking.
Irrelevant 0c	I got like that.	This is somebody's tree. Her foot look happy.	We have puzzles in the room.

Table B-19 *The following pattern of scoring was used for items in which there was an array of objects and the child had to select, label, or recall one or more objects from the array*

Score of 3 Fully Adequate	The child selects, labels, or recalls the correct object or objects.
Score of 2 Acceptable but Adds Extraneous	A correct response is offered but it includes extraneous material.
Score of 1 Ambiguous	The response is formulated in such a way that it is unclear as to whether it is correct or incorrect.
Score of 0 Inadequate* a	An inadequate response is offered.
b	
c	
d	
e	

*No hierarchy exists among the levels of the inadequate responses in this scoring pattern. Instead, multiple-choice items were involved, and a, b, c, d, and e indicate the choice the child made.

Table B-20   Scanning for an object

	Matching (cluster I-A)	Defined by Its Function (cluster II-A)	By Integrating Verbal with Visual Information (cluster III-A)
	(Find one like this.)	*(Find one that can . . . .)*	*(Find one to use with this.)*
Fully Adequate 3	Selects knife.	Selects knife, scissors, or paint scraper.	Selects knife.
Acceptable but Adds Extraneous 2	Selects knife plus one additional object.	Selects knife, scissors, or paint scraper plus one additional object.	Selects knife plus one additional object.
Ambiguous 1	↑	Not Applicable	↑
Inadequate 0a	Selects paintbrush, oranges, paint scraper, steak, pencil, or scissors.	Selects steak or oranges.	Selects paint scraper, scissors, or steak.
0b	Selects any objects not included in other categories.	Selects any objects not included in other categories.	Selects any objects not included in other categories.
0c	Selects random background material (i.e., nonsense figures).	Selects random background material.	Selects random background material.
0d	↓	Not Applicable	
0e	↓	Not Applicable	

Table B-21   Objects and characteristics

	By Sound (cluster I-B) (Show me what you heard.)	By Touch (cluster I-C) (Show me what you touched.)	Concepts: Attending to Two Characteristics (cluster II-G) (Find one that is . . . and . . . .)	Selecting the Means to a Goal (cluster IV-I) (What could we use?)
Fully Adequate 3	Selects bell.	Selects ball.	Selects cup that is upside down and has pictures.	Selects scissors.
Acceptable but Adds Extraneous 2	↓	Not Applicable		↑
Ambiguous 1	↓	Not Applicable		↑
Inadequate 0a	Selects whistle.	Selects pear.	Selects cup with small stripe.	Selects scotch tape.
0b	Selects rattle.	Selects yo-yo.	Selects cup with large stripe.	Selects outline of a star.
0c	Selects harmonica.	Selects styrofoam circle.	Selects cup that is upright and has pictures.	Selects one or all loose points of star.
0d	Not Applicable	Not Applicable	Selects small yellow cup.	Selects chalk.
0e				Selects arcs.

Table B-22 *Sequenced pictures*

Arranging Pictures in a Sequence
(cluster III-E)
(Make these into . . . .)

Fully Adequate* 3	Places pictures in following order from left to right: (a) a boy reaching for an apple; (b) boy bringing apple to his mouth; (c) boy holding apple with a bite taken from it; and (d) boy throwing core into trash can.
Acceptable but Adds Extraneous 2	Not Applicable
Ambiguous 1	Places pictures in correct order but sequence runs from right to left (2c/0a).
Inadequate 0a	Incorrectly orders pictures but the pictures are placed in a sequence with each picture placed in a vertical orientation.
0b	Not Applicable
0c	Makes no attempt to order pictures (i.e., twists pictures, places upside down, or uses fewer than four pictures).
0d	Places pictures exactly as presented.
0e	Not Applicable

*The categories for this item deviate somewhat from the scoring pattern outlined for multiple-choice type items. Since the sequence in which the pictures was placed was critical, this aspect is highlighted in the scoring.

Appendix C

Mean Percentage of Adequate Responses to Items in Each Process by Age and Socioeconomic Background

Table C-1   *Group I: Matching Perception*

Process	Number of Items	3 Year MC	3 Year LC	4 Year MC	4 Year LC	5 Year MC	5 Year LC
A. Scanning for a matching object	4	66		57		89	
			60		79		95
B. Identifying an object by sound	3	64		81		90	
			59		70		80
C. Identifying an object by touch	3	68		86		92	
			54		83		92
D. Naming an object heard	3	72		92		97	
			67		80		95
E. Naming an object touched	3	80		95		95	
			74		89		99
F. Naming an object seen	3	95		99		99	
			90		95		97
G. Imitating a simple sentence	6	81		97		99	
			67		92		96
H. Remembering pictorial object	4	52		64		82	
			51		67		81
I. Remembering incidental information	5	44		53		65	
			42		51		65

MC stands for middle class.
LC stands for lower class.

Table C-2   *Group II: Selective Analysis of Perception*

Process	Number of Items	3 Year MC	3 Year LC	4 Year MC	4 Year LC	5 Year MC	5 Year LC
A. Scanning for an object defined by its function	4	70	51	88	69	96	86
B. Describing a scene	2	51	41	64	60	79	66
C. Recalling items named in a statement	2	66	55	82	66	90	84
D. Recalling information from a statement	6	43	28	49	41	60	54
E. Completing a sentence	3	80	56	88	70	87	85
F. Concepts: Naming characteristics and functions of objects	9	74	51	86	71	94	88
G. Concepts: Attending to two characteristics	3	65	44	76	58	92	78
H. Concepts: Identifying differences	4	41	17	62	30	76	49
I. Concepts: Citing an example within a category	4	55	38	57	48	87	69

MC stands for middle class.
LC stands for lower class.

Table C-3   *Group III: Reordering Perception*

Process	Number of Items	3 Year MC	3 Year LC	4 Year MC	4 Year LC	5 Year MC	5 Year LC
A. Scanning for an object by integrating verbal with visual information	4	57	40	73	60	85	70
B. Describing events subsequent to a scene	2	43	31	70	51	72	69
C. Assuming the role of another person	5	57	28	56	58	72	73
D. Following a set of directions	2	64	54	74	58	76	63
E. Arranging pictures in a sequence	3	8	1	19	7	70	29
F. Formulating a set of directions	2	36	30	49	43	63	54
G. Formulating a generalization about a set of events	3	29	10	50	34	70	51
H. Formulating a statement to unify a sequence of pictures	2	34	8	61	43	76	52
I. Concepts: Identifying similarities	4	25	11	43	14	68	25
J. Concepts: Selecting an object by exclusion	2	64	30	82	51	93	72
K. Concepts: Selecting a set of objects by exclusion	4	31	5	67	25	80	52
L. Concepts: Citing an example by excluding a specific object	4	48	43	62	58	79	66
M. Concepts: Citing an example by excluding a class of objects	4	38	15	47	31	59	36
N. Concepts: Defining words	3	55	34	55	59	92	66
O. Unusual imitations	7	38	20	49	44	78	53

MC stands for middle class.
LC stands for lower class.

Table C-4   *Group IV: Reasoning about Perception*

Process	Number of Items	3 Year MC	3 Year LC	4 Year MC	4 Year LC	5 Year MC	5 Year LC
A. Predicting: Change in position	2	52	26	79	43	90	66
B. Predicting: Change in structure	5	54	34	70	60	80	74
C. Justifying a prediction	5	29	19	49	33	68	52
D. Justifying a decision: Essential characteristics	2	35	11	46	52	78	49
E. Justifying a Decision: Nonessential characteristics	2	16	6	25	6	55	22
F. Identifying the causes of an event	2	58	52	77	58	87	82
G. Formulating a solution	2	21	9	47	21	74	48
H. Formulating a solution from another's perspective	1	31	13	38	40	56	60
I. Selecting the means to a goal	4	44	21	64	40	80	56
J. Explaining the means to a goal	4	41	30	60	35	79	53
K. Explaining the construction of objects	3	23	3	45	29	83	43
L. Explaining an inference drawn from an observation	2	44	22	65	40	78	59
M. Explaining the logic of compound words	3	18	5	39	20	53	31
N. Explaining the obstacles to an action	6	44	15	66	42	79	56

MC stands for middle class.
LC stands for lower class.

Appendix D

Statistical Analyses

Table D-1   *Analysis of Variance of Children's Scores on the Four Groups of Items by Age, Socioeconomic Status, and Sex (total sample, N = 288)*

Source	df	MS	F
Between Subjects			
Age	2	71.11	128.92***
Class	1	48.26	87.48***
Sex	1	2.45	4.45*
Age x class	2	.05	1.0
Age x sex	2	.00	.00
Class x sex	1	.00	.00
Age x class x sex	2	.24	.43
Within Subjects			
Group I–IV scores	3	53.00	935.32***
Age x Score	6	.25	4.48***
Class x Score	3	2.70	47.56***
Sex x Score	3	.09	1.61
Age x Class x Score	6	.26	4.66***
Age x Sex x Score	6	.03	.54
Class x Sex x Score	3	.08	1.33
Age x Class x Sex x Score	6	.04	.74

*$p < .05$
***$p < .001$

Table D-2 *Analysis of Covariance of Children's Scores on the Four Groups of Items by Age, Socioeconomic Status, and Sex, with IQ as the Covariate (total sample, N = 288)*

Source	df	MS	F
Between Subjects			
Age	2	82.06	285.14***
Class	1	.82	2.86
Sex	1	.82	2.86
Age x Class	2	.20	7.0
Age x Sex	2	.13	.46
Class x Sex	1	.09	3.0
Age x Class x Sex	2	.31	1.06
Covariates	1	73.12	254.02***
Within Subjects			
Group I–IV scores	3	53.00	934.19***
Age x Scores	6	.25	4.48***
Class x Scores	3	2.70	47.50***
Sex x Scores	3	.09	1.61
Age x Class x Scores	6	.26	4.65
Age x Sex x Scores	6	.03	.54
Class x Sex x Scores	3	.08	1.33
Age x Class x Sex x Scores	6	.04	.74
Covariates	1	.00	.00

$***p < .001$

Table D-3 *Analysis of Variance of Children's Scores on the Four Groups of Items by Age and Socioeconomic Status (matched pairs sample, N = 90;† N = 45 pairs)*

Source	df	MS	F
Between Subjects			
Age	2	24.86	70.96***
Class	1	.03	.07
Age x Class	2	.12	.35
Within Subjects			
Group I–IV Scores	3	17.69	295.13***
Age x Scores	6	.26	4.26***
Class x Scores	3	.30	5.02**
Age x Class x Scores	6	.05	.79

†Matched for age, sex, and IQ.
$**p < .005$
$***p < .001$

Appendix E

Illustrations of Discourse Demands in Teaching

This appendix represents an elaboration of the ideas raised in Chapter 6 in the section on accommodating children's skills. There we emphasized that the content of any curriculum could be transmitted to the children if the teacher's verbalizations were phrased within the discourse demands already mastered by them. This appendix is designed to illustrate this concept more fully by taking four activities typically used for teaching young children and then showing how each group of discourse demands (Groups I, II, III, or IV) can be introduced into these activities. In the actual teaching, the various levels should be interwoven. For purposes of exposition, however, they are presented in separate blocks (e.g., all Group I demands, then all Group II demands, and so forth). The activities that we have chosen for this purpose are a cooking lesson, an art activity, story time, and music. A fully sequenced dialogue is not presented in any of these lessons. Rather, some key demands from each group of discourse skills are presented to illustrate the range of ideas that can be encompassed.

A Cooking Activity: The activity here is making chocolate pudding.
Group I demands
The teacher has shown a child one box of chocolate pudding. The teacher tells the child that they need a second box and asks the child to:

1. "Find one just like the one we have." (On the table is an array of objects composed of things such as cooking implements, foods, and silverware.)
2. While the boxes are out of the child's view, the teacher asks, "What pictures did you see on the box?"
3. The teacher picks up a spoon to mix the pudding and says, "What do we call this?"
4. The teacher tells the child that they have to add some milk to the pudding and says, "Please go get the milk."

Group II demands

1. The teacher asks the child to close his eyes and feel the dry chocolate powder. The teacher then asks, "How does that feel?" (This is an example of how a Group I demand, that is, identifying an object by touch, can be extended to Group II, that is, naming characteristics of objects.)
2. The child says that the pudding is ready and the teacher says, "Fine, but we need to put it in something so we can each eat some. Find something over there [pointing out to child an array of objects] that we could use so that we could each have some pudding."
3. The teacher reads some of the instructions on the box (e.g., "It says, pour two cups of milk into the contents") and then asks, "How many cups did it say?"
4. While the child is mixing the pudding mixture with the spoon, the teacher asks, "What are you doing now?"

Group III demands

1. While the child is mixing the pudding, the teacher asks, "If we hadn't had a spoon to mix this with, what other thing could we have used?"
2. At the beginning of the lesson before any materials are introduced, the teacher says, "We're going to make some pudding just like some we had at lunch the other day. Can you tell me what pudding is ?"
3. The child begins to speak about foods that he likes (e.g., cookies), and the teacher says, "What's the same about cookies and pudding?"
4. While the child is spooning the pudding mixture out the teacher asks, "What will we do with the bowl after we have taken out all the pudding?"

Group IV demands

1. The child, on seeing the box of pudding, declares, "There was chocolate pudding inside." The teacher then asks, "How could you tell that pudding was in this box?"
2. After the dry (powdery) pudding is placed into a bowl, the teacher asks, "If we add some milk to this, what will happen to the pudding?"
3. While the child is spooning the completed pudding into bowls, the teacher asks, "Why shouldn't we use a fork to do that instead of a spoon?"
4. While the teacher and child are eating the pudding, the teacher comments, "They put sugar in the pudding. Why do you think they put sugar in?"

An Art Activity: The activity here is making a collage.
Group I demands

1. The teacher says, "We need some paper to draw with. Please go to the closet and get some paper."
2. When the child returns to the table from the closet the teacher asks, "Were there other sheets of paper in the closet?"
3. The teacher and child are sitting at the table. The teacher says, "Look at all of these things. There are so many—paper, pencils, crayons, scissors. Close your eyes; keep them closed. Now feel the things on the table and find the scissors.

4. As the teacher and child are mixing paints to use to color the background, the teacher holds up a red jar of paint and says to the child, "Go over to the easel, and find another jar that looks just like this one."

Group II demands

1. There is an array of art supplies on the table, including tape, glue, scissors, crayons, and several paint brushes of different sizes and colors. The teacher says to the child, "Let's use the paint brush that's big and has a green handle. Find that one."
2. In talking about the pasting of the collage, the teacher asks, "What thing could we use to put the paste onto the paper so our hands won't get dirty?"
3. While cutting out pieces for the collage, the teacher talks about hanging the child's work on the wall after it's completed. She says to the child, "I'd like to hang your collage up when you're finished with it. Go over to the table and find me something we could hang the collage up on the wall with."
4. While the child is examining all the supplies on the table the teacher says, "Name all of the things on the table that we can use for drawing a picture."

Group III demands

1. As the child has finished her collage, the teacher says, "Tell me all the things we did to make this collage."
2. As the child is working on pasting all the different shapes onto another paper, teacher says to her, "Point out all the shapes that are *not* squares" (on her collage).
3. As the child uses the paints, the teacher points to the table (which has an array of art materials on it, including crayons, pencils, paper, and sticks) and says, "Point out something else we could draw with if we had no paints."
4. After the collage has been completed, the teacher says, "If you wanted to tell your mother what your collage looks like, what would you say about it?"

Group IV demands

1. When the teacher sends the child to get supplies from the closet at the onset of the lesson, the paint jars are up on a high shelf. The child has difficulty trying to get them, and the teacher says, "How come you can't reach the paints?"
2. The teacher tells the child that he would like to put her collage up on the wall and he asks her, "What could we use so that your collage will stay up on the wall?"
3. After the child has indicated which side of the tape ought to be put on the paper, the teacher asks, "Why shouldn't we put this side [the nonsticky side] on the paper?"
4. While the child is using the paint brush to color her collage, the teacher asks, "Why do we have to clean the brushes in water each time we use a different color?"

Story Time: The activity here is reading a book.
The teacher is reading a book such as *Are You My Mother?* to the children.

This is a tale of a baby bird who hatches and has "lost" his mother. The baby bird goes in search of his mother and encounters all sorts of people and things in the world.

Group I demands

1. The teacher brings out the book and tells the child that they are going to read it. She then asks the child to open the book.
2. After examining the back cover with the child, the teacher asks, "Is there a picture here?"
3. After naming several pictures on the cover and first page, the child turns the pages to continue the story. The teacher says to the child, "Before we read this next part, tell me some of the things you saw so far."
4. As they read the story, the teacher and child talk about the baby bird hatching in his nest. They make a nest out of cotton and enact part of the story. While constructing the nest the teacher asks the child to close her eyes and feel first the cotton and then some twigs. The teacher says, "Feel this. Now feel this. Okay, now give me the one that is cotton."

Group II demands

1. While the child is turning the cover, the teacher points to it and says, "What is this part of the book called?"
2. The bird continues to search for his mother in the book. Of each person or thing he meets, he asks, "Are you my mother?" When the part of the book in which the baby bird meets an airplane is reached, the teacher asks the child, "How are the bird and the airplane different?"
3. The teacher says, "Now he comes to a cat and says, "Are you my————?"
4. At the beginning of the story as the bird is slowly hatching and the shell of the egg is cracking, the teacher says, "What's happening on this page now?"

Group III demands

1. As the teacher and child turn the page, they get to a picture of the bird meeting a tractor. The teacher says to child, "What do you think the baby bird will say to the tractor?"
2. While reading, the child makes a comment that sometimes children also get lost. The teacher asks, "What does it mean to be lost?"
3. When the baby bird finally discovers his mother, the teacher points to the two and asks the child, "How are the mother and the baby bird the same?"
4. The teacher says, "Tell me three things that the baby bird met that weren't animals."

Group IV demands

1. At the start of the book, before the bird has hatched from the egg, the teacher and child have agreed that the baby bird in the shell could not see things outside his shell. The teacher asks, "Why can't he see anything when he's inside the shell?"

2. The teacher and child have set up a reconstruction of an egg in a nest of cotton to enact part of the story. The child is talking about the bird coming out of the egg with his beak showing as the egg begins to crack. The teacher says, "Why does he use his beak to break the shell?"
3. The teacher and child have been talking about the color of the shell. The teacher asks, "Could the baby bird have broken the shell if it had been blue instead of white?"
4. The teacher reads that the baby bird is too young to fly, but that he is going to try. She shows the picture of the bird in the tree to the child and asks her, "What will happen when he tries to fly?"

Music Lesson: The activity here is learning about musical instruments.
Group I demands

1. The teacher and child are going to engage in a lesson centered on musical instruments. The teacher selects a tambourine and says, "This has these things that move [pointing to metal discs]. Look [he moves them]. You do that."
2. There is an array of objects, only one of which can make a noise. Teacher says, "Close your eyes and listen [he rings the bell]." He then says, "Now, open your eyes. Tell me which thing made that noise?"
3. After having played the instruments, the teacher collects all of them. He then asks, "Which are some of the instruments that we played today?"
4. The teacher points to a drum in the array and asks the child, "Tell me what this is called."

Group II demands

1. While selecting different types of instruments to play, the teacher says to one child, "Look for an instrument that you have to use with sticks."
2. The teacher says, "Listen, I'm going to make some sounds with these." The teacher bangs one drum firmly and another drum gently and then asks, "Which sound was louder?"
3. After playing several instruments, the teacher says, "Which ones did we have to play with our mouths?"
4. After the child tries several instruments, the teacher says, "Find an instrument that you play with both your mouth and your hands."

Group III demands

1. The teacher says, "Let's make a record of the instruments that we played." (Small pictures of the instruments being used are available.) "Here, I'll tap the drum and then ring the bell. Now I'll put those pictures here because those are things that I used. Now, you use two instruments and then use the pictures to show what you did."
2. The teacher says, "Let's leave the drum and xylophone here and just pretend you were holding them. Then show me what you would do if you were playing the drum and if you were playing the xylophone."

3. The teacher has four instruments out (a drum, a xylophone, a bell, and a trumpet). He says, "I'm going to play three of these in a row." The teacher then rings the bell, taps the drum, and plays the xylophone and says, "Now, you play the ones that I did and do it in the same order."
4. The teacher says to the child, "Find me something in this room that makes noise but is not a musical instrument."

Group IV demands

1. The teacher and child examine two bells, one with and one without a clapper, and they see that one works and one doesn't. The teacher says, "Why does this work and this one doesn't?"
2. The teacher asks the child, "If we held the clapper while we were shaking this bell, would it ring? Why?"
3. After the child has selected the parts necessary to make a xylophone, the teacher asks, "How will we put these things together?"
4. The teacher asks, "If we didn't have the sticks for the drum, what could we use to get the drum to make noise?"

References

Allen D: The development of prediction in child language. Unpublished doctoral dissertation, Teachers College, Columbia University, 1973

Altus W D: Birth order and its sequalae. Science 151: 44–59, 1966

Amidon E J, Hough J B (eds): Interaction analysis: Theory, Research, and Application. Reading, Mass., Addison-Wesley, 1967

Anastasi A: Psychological testing. New York, Macmillan, 1961

Banet B: Toward a developmentally valid preschool curriculum. High/Scope, Educational Research Foundation Report, Ypsilanti, Michigan, 1975.

Barnes D: Language in the secondary classroom, in Barnes D, Britton J, Rosen H (eds): Language, the Learner and the School. Harmondsworth, England, Penguin, 1969

Barnes D, Britton J, Rosen H: (eds) Language, the Learner and the School. Harmondsworth, England, Penguin, 1969

Bates E: Pragmatics and sociolinguistics in child language, in Morehead D M, Morehead A E (eds): Normal and Deficient Child Language. Baltimore, University Park Press, 1976

Bellack A A, Kliebard H M, Hyman R T, Smith F L, Jr: The Language of the Classroom. New York, Teachers College Press, 1966

Beller E K: Research on organized programs of early education, in Travers R M W (ed): Second Handbook of Research on Teaching. Skokie, Ill., Rand McNally, 1973

Bennett S N, Jordon J: A typology of teaching styles in primary schools. Br J Educ Psychol 45: 20–28, 1975

Bereiter C, Englemann S: Teaching Disadvantaged Children in the Preschool. Englewood Cliffs, N. J., Prentice-Hall, 1966

Binet A, Simon T: The Development of Intelligence in Children (Kite E S, trans). Baltimore, Williams & Wilkins, 1916

Blank M: The wrong response: Is it to be ignored, prevented, or treated?, in Parker R K (ed): Preschool in Action. Boston, Allyn & Bacon, 1972

———: Teaching Learning in the Preschool: A Dialogue Approach. Columbus, Ohio, Charles E. Merrill, 1973

———: Cognitive functions of language in the preschool years. Dev Psychol 10: 229–245, 1974

———:Eliciting verbalization from young children in experimental tasks: A methodological note. Child Dev 46: 254–257, 1975

———: Language, the child and the teacher: A proposed assessment model, in Hom H L, Robinson P (eds): Psychological Processes in Early Childhood. New York, Academic Press, 1977

Blank M, Allen D A: Understanding "Why": Its significance in early intelligence, in Lewis M (ed): Origins of Intelligence: Infancy and Early Childhood. New York, Plenum Press, 1976

Blank M, Koltuv M, Wood M: Individual teaching for disadvantaged kindergarten children: A comparison of two methods. J Spec Educ 6: 207–219, 1972

Blank M, Solomon F: A tutorial language program to develop abstract thinking in socially disadvantaged pre-school children. Child Dev 39: 379–389, 1968

———, ———: How shall the disadvantaged child be taught? Child Dev 40: 47–61, 1969

Bloom B S: Recent developments in mastery learning. Educ Psychol 10: 53–57, 1973

Bloom L, Rocissano L, Hood L: Adult–child discourse: Developmental interaction between information processing and linguistic knowledge. Cognitive Psychol 8: 521–552, 1976

Bowerman M: Semantic factors in the acquisition of rules for word use and sentence construction, in Morehead D M, Morehead A E (eds): Normal and Deficient Child Language. Baltimore, University Park Press, 1976

———: Discussion summary: Development of concepts underlying language, in Schiefelbush R L, Lloyd L L (eds): Language Perspectives: Acquisition, Retardation, and Intervention. Baltimore, University Park Press, 1974

Broman S H, Nichols P L, Kennedy W A: Preschool IQ; Prenatal and early developmental correlates. Hillsdale, N.J., Lawrence Erlbaum, 1975

Brown R: Introduction to Moffett J: Teaching the Universe of Discourse. Boston, Houghton Mifflin, 1968a

———: The development of WH questions in child speech. J Verbal Learning Behav 7:279–290, 1968b

———: A First Language: The Early Stages. Cambridge, Mass., Harvard University Press, 1973

Bruck M, Tucker G R: Social class differences in the acquisition of school language. Merrill-Palmer Q 20: 205–220, 1974

Bryant P: Perception and Understanding in Young Children. New York, Basic Books, 1975

Candlin C N: Sociolinguistics and communicative language teaching. ITL 16: 37–44, 1972

Cazden C B: Child Language and Education. New York, Holt, Rinehart & Winston, 1972

————: Play with language and metalinguistic awareness: One dimension of language experience. Paper presented at The Second Lucy Sprague Memorial Conference Dimensions of Language Experience. Bank Street College of Education, 1973a

————: Problems for education: Language as curriculum content and learning environment. Daedalus 102: 135–148, 1973b

Cazden C B, John V P, Hymes D (eds): Functions of Language in the Classroom. New York, Teachers College Press, 1972

Charlesworth W R: Surprise and cognitive development, in Elkind D, Flavell J H (eds): Studies in Cognitive Development: Essays in Honor of Jean Piaget. New York, Oxford University Press, 1969

Chrelashviti N V: On a critical moment in the child's mental (speech) development. Early Child Dev Care 1: 197–205, 1972

Chukovsky K: From Two to Five. (Morton M. trans, ed) Berkeley, University of California Press, 1963

Coulthard M: Approaches to the analysis of classroom interaction. Educ Rev 26: 229–240, 1974

Criper C, Davies A: Research on spoken language in the primary school, in Davies A (ed): Language and Learning in Early Childhood. London, Heinemann, 1977

Dale P S: Language Development: Structure and Function. Hinsdale, Ill., Dryden Press, 1972

Deutsch M, Jensen A R, Katz I: Social-Class, Race, and Psychological Development. New York, Holt, Rinehart & Winston, 1968

Donaldson M, Wales R: On the acquisition of some relational terms, in Hayes J R (ed): Cognition and the Development of Language. New York, Wiley, 1970

Dreger R M, Miller K S: Comparative psychological studies of negroes and whites in the United States. Psychol Bull 57: 361–402, 1960

Eimas P D: Speech perception in early infancy, in Cohen L B, Salapatek P (ed): Infant Perception. New York, Academic Press, 1975

Ervin-Tripp S: Discourse agreement: How children answer questions, in Hayes J R (ed): Cognition and the Development of Language. New York, Wiley, 1970

Fahey G L: The questioning activity of children. J Genet Psychol 60: 337–357, 1942

Fantz R L: The origin of form perception. Sci Am 204: 66–72, 1961

Flanders N A: Analyzing teacher behavior. Reading, Mass., Addison-Wesley, 1970

Gagné R M: The Conditions of Learning (ed 2). New York, Holt, Rinehart & Winston, 1970

Garvey C: Play, in Bruner J, Cole M, Lloyd B (gen eds): The Developing Child series. Cambridge, Mass: Harvard University Press, 1977

Garvey C, Hogan R: Social speech and social interaction: Egocentricism revisited. Child Dev 44: 562–568, 1973

Gelman R: Early number concepts, in Reese H W (ed): Advances in Child Development and Behavior, vol. 7. New York, Academic Press, 1972

Glaser R: Instructional technology and the measurement of learning outcomes. Am Psychol 18: 519–521, 1963

————: Educational psychology and education. Am Psychol 28: 557–566, 1973

————: The processes of intelligence and education, in Resnick L B (ed): The Nature of Intelligence. Hillsdale, N. J., Lawrence Erlbaum, 1976, pp 341–352

Glaser R, Nitko A J: Measurement in learning and instruction, in Thorndike R L (ed): Educational Measurement (ed 2). Washington, D. C., American Council on Education, 1971

Gleitman L, Rozin P: Teaching reading by use of a syllabary. Reading Res Q 3: 447–483, 1973

Goodnow J J: Compensation arguments on conservation tasks. Dev Psychol 8: 140, 1973

Gordon I J, Jester R E: Techniques of observing teaching in early childhood, in Travers R M W (ed): Second Handbook of Research on Teaching. Skokie, Ill., Rand McNally, 1973

Haith M, Kessen R, Collins D: Responses of the human infant to level of complexity of intermittent visual movement. J Exp Child Psychol 7: 52–69, 1969

Higgins E T: Social class differences in verbal communicative accuracy: A question of "which question?" Psychol Bull 83: 695–714, 1976

Hollingshead A B, Redlich F C: Social Class and Mental Illness: A Community Study, New York, Wiley, 1958, pp 390–391

Isaacs S: Intellectual Growth in Young Children. London, George Routledge, 1930

Jensen A R: Educability and group differences. New York, Harper & Row, 1973

Kearsley G P: Questions and question asking in verbal discourse: A cross-disciplinary review. J Psychololinguis Res, 1976, 5, 355–375

Kohnstamm G A: Piaget's Analyses of Class Inclusion: Right or Wrong. The Hague: Mouton, 1967

Krasner W: Children's play and social speech. An NIMH program report, U.S. Dept. HEW Research grant MH-23883, September 1975

Krauss R M, Glucksberg S: The development of communication: Competence as a function of age. Child Dev 40: 255–256, 1969

Kuhn T S: The Structure of Scientific Revolutions. Chicago, University of Chicago Press, 1962

Labov W: The logic of non-standard English, in Alatis J A (ed): Linguistics and the Teaching of Standard English. Monograph Series of Language and Linguistics, No. 22. Washington, D.C., Georgetown University Press, 1969

Lawton D: Social Class, Language, and Education. London, Routledge & Kegan Paul, 1968

Lewis M M: Infant Speech (ed 2). London, Routledge & Kegan Paul, 1951

Liberman I: Segmentation of the spoken word and reading acquisition. Paper presented at the Symposium on Language and Perceptual Development in the Acquisition of Reading, Society for Research in Child Development, Philadelphia, March 1973

Loehlin J C, Lindzey G, Spuhler J N: Race Differences in Intelligence. San Francisco, W. H. Freeman, 1975

Luria A R: Verbal regulation of behavior, in Brazier M A B (ed): Signal Systems and the Development of Cognitive Functions: The Central Nervous System and Behavior. Transactions of New York Third Conference Josiah Macy, Jr. Foundation, 1960

————: The Role of Speech in the Regulation of Normal and Abnormal Behavior. New York, Pergamon, 1961

Maccoby E E, Jacklin C N: The Psychology of Sex Differences. Stanford, Stanford University Press, 1974

Macnamara J: Cognitive basis of language learning in infants. Psychol Rev 79: 1–14, 1972

McNeil J D, Popham W J: The assessment of teacher competence, in Travers R M W (ed): Second Handbook of Research on Teaching. Skokie, Ill., Rand McNally, 1973

Mercer J R: Labeling the Mentally Retarded. Berkeley, University of California Press, 1973

Miller L B, Dyer J L: Four preschool programs: Their dimensions and effects. Monogr Soc Res Child Dev 40: 1–170, 1975

Moffet J: Teaching the Universe of Discourse. Boston, Houghton Mifflin, 1968

Mueller E: The maintenance of verbal exchanges between young children. Child Dev 43: 930–938, 1972

Nelson K: Concept, word, and sentence: Interrelations in acquisition and development. Psychol Rev 81: 267–285, 1974

Olson P A: Introduction: The craft of teaching and the school of teachers. Report of the First National Conference. U. S. Office of Education, Denver, Tri-University Project in Elementary Education, September 1967

Parker R K (ed): The Preschool in Action. Boston, Allyn & Bacon, 1972

Piaget J: Play, Dreams and Imitation in Childhood (Gattegno C, Hodgson F M, trans) London, Heinemann, 1951

————: The Origins of Intelligence in Children. New York, International Universities Press, 1952

————: Genetic epistemology. Forum 12: 4–11, 1969

Robison H F: Exploring Teaching in Early Childhood Education. Boston, Allyn & Bacon, 1977

Rose S A, Blank M: The potency of context in children's cognition: An illustration through conservation. Child Dev 45: 499–502, 1974

Satz P, Sparrow S S: Specific developmental dyslexia: A theoretical formulation, in Baker D J, Satz P (eds): Specific Reading Disability: Advances in Theory and Method. Rotterdam: Rotterdam University Press, 1970

Scandura J M: Structural approach to instructional problems. Am Psychol 32: 33–53, 1977

Schatz M, Gelman R: The development of communication skills: Modifications in the speech of young children as a function of the listener. Monogr Soc Res Child Dev 38: 1–38, 1973

Schlesinger I M: Relational concepts underlying language, in Schiefelbusch R L, Lloyd L L (eds): Language Perspectives: Acquisition, Retardation and Intervention. Baltimore, University Park Press, 1974

Shantz C U, Watson J S: Assessment of spatial egocentrism through expectancy violation. Psychonom Sci 18: 93–94, 1970

Sigel I E: The search for validity or the evaluator's nightmare, in Weinberg R A, Moore S G (eds): Evaluation of Educational Programs for Young Children. Washington, D.C., Child Development Associate Consortium, 1975

Sigel I E, Cocking R R: Cognition and communication: A dialectic paradigm for development, in Lewis M, Rosenblum L A (eds): Interaction, Conversation and the Development of Language. New York, Wiley, 1977

Simon A, Boyer E (eds): Mirrors for behavior: An anthology of classroom observation instruments. Classroom Interaction Newsletter, 3, 1968

Soar R S, Soar R M: An attempt to identify measures of teacher effectiveness from four studies. Paper presented at the American Educational Research Association meeting. San Francisco, April 1976

Stevenson H W: Children's Learning. Englewood Cliffs, N.J., Prentice-Hall, 1972

Stone L J, Smith H T, Murphy L B (eds): The Competent Infant. New York, Basic Books, 1973

Taba H: Teaching strategies and cognitive functioning in elementary school children. U.S. OE Cooperative Research Project No. 2404. San Francisco, San Francisco State College, 1966

Taba H, Elkins D: Teaching Strategies for the Culturally Disadvantaged. Skokie, Ill., Rand McNally, 1966

Thorndike R L: Renormed IQ test shows kids are smarter. Spec Educ Newsletter 14: 32–33, 1976

Tough J: The Development of Meaning: A Study of Children's Use of Language. New York, Wiley, 1977

Trabasso T, Nicholas D A, Omanson R, Johnson L: Inferences and story comprehension. Paper for the Symposium on the Development of Discourse Processing Skills. Society for Research in Child Development Meetings. New Orleans, March 1977

Zajonc R B: Family configuration and intelligence. Science 192: 227–236, 1976

Zaporozhets A V, Elkonin D B (eds): The Psychology of Preschool Children (Shybut J, Simon S, trans). Cambridge, Mass., MIT Press, 1971

Indexes

Author Index

Subject Index

a
b
c
d
e
8 f
9 g
0 h
1 i
8 2 j